POWERFUL
CHOICES
FOR MID-CAREER WOMEN

How to Create Your Personal Pathway
to Meaning, Prosperity and Your Next Great Job

Phyllis Horner, PhD

Powerful Choices for Mid-Career Women –

How to Create Your Personal Pathway to Meaning, Prosperity and Your Next Great Job

Copyright: © Phyllis C. Horner

Published: November 23, 2015

ISBN: 978-1-941832-02-8

Publisher: Wisdom Media International LLC

Your Route, Your Speed, Your Style™ is an active Service Mark.

Want to know more? Go to https://wisdommedia.leadpages.co/your-career-age/

You can also find out more about the author and upcoming books online at www.phyllishorner.com or contact her at thrivingcareer@gmail.com

Contact Info:

Phyllis Horner
Career Excelerator LLC
P.O. Box 25914
Honolulu, HI 96825

Dedicated to my husband, Manny, our beautiful and strong daughters Lani and Lena, my family and friends, and to all the inspiring women who have had the courage and talent to tackle the world of work.

Contents

Read Me First!

There are many books emerging on mid- to late careers because of the sheer number of us (currently estimated at 20% or more of the population) who are near 50 years old and may never retire in the traditional sense of our parent's generation. Women, especially, are considering working longer. Some of us are just too "young" while others fear living alone and becoming poor. But, for the most part, these are the overt signs of something deeper. Many of us fear retirement because it signals the end of vibrancy, influence, and making a visible difference in the world. And for our generation, which started with Woodstock/Age of Aquarius and war protests, it has been extremely important to our self-image that our opinions loudly shape the world.

Now, we still wear skinny jeans and pursue extreme sports, as long as we possibly can—we crave youthfulness and deny the aging process like none before us. Modern medicine and a lifetime of fitness and good nutrition (not to mention cosmetic surgery) have supported our efforts to stay "in the fast lane."

In writing this book, I'm assuming you are a professional woman, approximately between 45 and 60 years old, but whatever your age, you have a lot of time left to work. Use this book to plan what you want to do with the next 20 or more years of your life. This book is dedicated to your self-exploration of your options for the future, of data to put things in perspective, and of a way to look at working (a little or a lot) as a good thing, at least as good as what we thought retirement would be for us in the "old school American Dream."

The metaphor of being in the driver's seat of your career and viewing work as a "vehicle" for self-expression in the world helps us to see that no matter how seriously we take any given job, we find meaning from it to the extent it matches our personal values and goals.

The good news is that for the first time in your career, you actually have more options to do what you want to do than ever before. The fact that there are fewer available workers in current generations (X, Y, and Millennials) than in ours leads to opportunity for us. Plus, there is a generalized worry by employers that our generation will not be replaceable at the same rate that we will leave the workforce.

A little about my qualifications to write this book:

First, I am a youngish boomer myself. I am one of the 50+ percent of our generation who has been divorced and needed to start over financially. I live in one of the most expensive cost-of-living states, where people live long and where most employers don't provide fixed pensions. I am also by training an organizational psychologist focused on career transitions, change management, and human resources. I have worked inside large (Fortune 5) companies and for mid-sized businesses, for not-for-profit organizations, and for myself as a solopreneur leadership and strategy consultant.

I've left the workforce a couple of times because of personal priorities and then reentered. I moved four times inter-state for my career, and each time had to rebuild my brand and establish my network and value. I have lived alone as well as been married twice, knowing the impact of those lifestyles both financially and otherwise. I'm certified to interpret several personality assessments, as well as change management, personal branding, and a values assessment. I have taught hundreds of workshops and had about that many career and executive coaching clients in about 30 years of professional work. And I am not exempt from career stress—I understand what it's like myself and live it daily.

In this easy and fun guide you will have the chance to rethink your values and goals as they apply to work, to put work into the overall context of your life goals, and even to match your personality and preferred work style to the next type of job you seek. The assumption is that even if you choose to walk away from the "cubicle or corner office" life, that some form of productive work will engage your mind and heart for decades to come.

So let's get started.

Introduction

Women's Mid-Career Planning Is Special

If you, like me, are over 45 years old with a lot of road to travel between now and when you are "retirement eligible" in your mid-60s, you may wake up often and wonder how you should best spend those years to minimize stress while maximizing meaning and prosperity. If so, you're not alone. Over 60% of women are worried about the end of their careers, even while still in the middle of them. Many of us feel, for the first time, like time is running out to do what we really love for pay, so we can feel trapped by staying on our current path if it is less than satisfactory.

Logic tells us that we shouldn't feel this way, that with 20+ years of work left for most of us, we should expect several more jobs to "come our way." But therein lies the problem. Once over 50, many of us feel vulnerable when it comes to finding a new job—any job—not even thinking of one that fills us with joy and fulfillment. If you want to get a free resource that helps you get great insight into "Your Real Career Age" vs. your age in years, go to www.phyllishorner.com.

Even though the AARP and other groups speak of how successful people navigate from mid-career to encore careers, they don't really address the planning process in an in-depth way. A big untapped part of the planning process is moving from what we are good at to what we love at this point in our lives, without giving up security and status.

This book is dedicated to helping mid-career women build up their readiness for multi-dimensional planning that considers intellectual challenge, energy and interest, spirit and meaning, and security and physical well-being. For women, our well-being has always been a multidimensional thing, including service to a larger goal and being part of valuable relationships.

As an experienced career coach helping others escape from unhappy work lives into jobs with better fit, money, and lifestyle, I've not only studied all the major career approaches and helped others use them, but experimented with many of them myself.

We can joyfully and confidently move forward to multiple new jobs by taking stock of our strengths and interests, sorting out our fears, doubts, and confusion, and claiming new jobs that use our natural talents while allowing us less stress. It's possible once you have a game plan.

Throughout the book you will have choices to make—and links to research. In the end, you will be the one to determine whether the path forward is likely to be filled with 2, 3, 4, or more new jobs, as you transition from upward to onward. And you'll be able to predict at when you may want to take on big new challenges or, alternatively, take a less stressful path.

A big insight for many of us is that what we have worked so hard to achieve is not as meaningful as it was in prior years— many feel itchy for something new. Reported in the

Huffington Post, 54 percent of people age 40+ are currently seeking to change jobs but feel significant barriers to do so.[1]

A solution to this dilemma, in addition to creating multiple scenarios for your future work, is to view the time left as a less traditional career, one where you are not expected to do the same things in a particular order, and where you can change as often as you wish. Looking at a series of jobs you are interested in and talented for frees your spirit and keeps you employed at the same time. It frees you from the model of worklife you have carried around in your head for several decades. This is a huge benefit because once you create a new view of your work, you can also make plans for other aspects of life that you want to develop more fully. It protects you from thinking that one plan will work for the next 20 years, which rarely occurs. Finally, it gives you multiple options to consider over those years, so that you do not need any one job or situation to work out.

The main premise is that it is powerful and smart to look at jobs after mid-career mainly as a context for what you still want to learn and do in your life. You are the one to decide your destination. You decide the route, the speed, and how it fits your style. Accepting that you determine the destination is your key to success. And mid-career is the

---

[1] 1. Harris Poll conducted for University of Phoenix, April 2013. http://www.huffingtonpost.com/2013/07/01/workers-change-careers_n_3530346.html

perfect time to rethink and choose new destinations to keep yourself young, interested, and growing.

The book uses a "steering wheel" model, organized into three phases:

- Prepare for Your New Journeys
- Create Your Mid-Career Roadmap, and
- Use Your Roadmap.

It's a fun, easy, and specific model to build your ability to keep your "hands on the wheel" for the rest of your career.

The first phase, *Prepare for New Journeys*, includes knowing how to handle the mid-career "crossroads," thinking about where you've been, what you liked and hated, and how you are feeling about your current situation. To fully prepare for new journeys, you need to "harvest" information about your past and present jobs and skills, and get past doubting yourself to realize this new phase of worklife is a great opportunity to accept the pull to something new.

The second phase shows you how to *Create Your Mid-Career Roadmap*. This phase includes pulling together information about how you define success at work going forward, including what gives you meaning from a whole-person perspective. We use a concept called "Career MPG"— meaning, prosperity, and growth—because knowing what you value gives you power in your future planning. Setting boundaries on what you want to do, what natural talents you have to do it, how much money you need to make, and the ideal working conditions that match your preferences together create a powerful intended direction. Your roadmap for future jobs will need to match your style, your route, and your other preferences, including the following:

- Your personality
- Your natural talents
- What gives you meaning, your values
- Your interests
- Money, benefits, and security
- Your schedule and work environment
- Manageable or reduced stress levels

The third phase is *Use Your Roadmap*, which includes mid- and short-term goals, planning for research or networking that needs to happen, and learning how to communicate your goals to others.

To use your roadmap, you have to determine your desired destinations and then several job options that lead toward the destination. Even though you are at mid-career, I encourage you to plan "with the end of work in mind." That will ensure you have peace of mind as you take the next steps forward.

I promise that if you use the information and planning in this guide, you will untangle any confusion and understand your strengths well enough to chart a joyful, superb route to future career success for many years to come.

The chart below shows the phases and their corresponding action steps. By following each action in order, you will build a clear confidence that will enable you to move past barriers, both internal and external, and create a meaningful, joyful rest of your worklife.

Phase	Areas of Exploration
1 – Prepare for New Journeys	**PART 1:** Master the Crossroads **PART 2:** Past – Looking back to move forward **PART 3:** Present – Assess your current job **PART 4:** Decide – Commit to move forward Summary: Roadblocks and Accelerators
2 – Create Your Mid-Career Roadmap	**PART 1:** Your Unique Style Your Personality and Ideal Work Your Natural Skills and Talents Your MPG – Meaning, prosperity, and growth **PART 2:** Pull It All Together Your Preferred Routes – How to decide Your Turn – Summarize your unique style and preferred routes Roadmap Research Summary: Roadblocks and Accelerators
3 – Use Your Roadmap	**PART 1:** Getting Ready To Use Your Roadmap Acquire the Courage To Act **PART 2:** Short-Term Actions To Move Forward **PART 3:** Use the "Rules of the Road" Summary: Roadblock and Accelerators Conclusion

Phase 1 –
Prepare for New Journeys

To prepare ourselves to make what may seem like risky moves at a vulnerable time of life, we need to learn from ourselves, from the wisest part of us that knows what we are capable of and what would really bring us joy while sustaining us monetarily. Luckily, it's easy to do. We just need to look backward and pull forward our learning from prior jobs and times of life. This is one of the best parts of mid-career planning as opposed to earlier planning. The first part is *Mastering the Crossroads.*

1 – Prepare for New Journeys	**PART 1**: Master the Crossroads **PART 2**: Past – Looking back to move forward **PART 3**: Present – Assess your current job **PART 4**: Decide – Commit to move forward Summary: Roadblocks and Accelerators

PART 1 -
Mastering The Crossroads

We're going to look at this phase through the eyes of another talented woman, who we'll call Debbie.

Debbie's Dilemma

Debbie was just going through the motions at work. She had just turned 57 when she realized abruptly that she would need to continue to work indefinitely, perhaps past "retirement age". Her longtime partner had recently left, and she knew she was going to have to find her own way, once again, in the world. She was a skilled computer programmer in her youth, someone who had been there at the early days of the computer revolution. Over time she had kept up with all the changes, which allowed her to have a good income and a sense of accomplishment. About 10 years ago, she was promoted to group leader for IT in the mid-sized hospitality business where she had worked for 15 years.

She missed the actual programming work, but she got a sense of joy watching her people grow and stretch their wings. That is, until last year. After she and her husband split up, she felt like she was starting anew, and she was unsettled, so things that used to seem normal now made her nervous. She found work a chore and became worried that she was stuck in her job. She kept on with it for security reasons even though the joy of the work had faded, and she hated herself for that too. She didn't know which way to turn, but she knew if she didn't make a change soon, she would lose her sense of purpose.

Debbie is a composite of the pressures, emotions, and circumstances that many of us find ourselves in at mid-career. We are too old and too young—too young to retire, too old to easily start anew. Many of us probably left our roles of actually performing the work and instead guide that work as managers and leaders now, roles which for many are less fulfilling and more stressful. And, like Debbie, we have had to contend with the normal life stressors that come along, usually at inconvenient times. We find ourselves without good role models for how to get out of our situation without just substituting one set of problems for another.

Like Debbie, many of us have found our own way, but the rules of how to move forward successfully from mid-career to the end of a career have been changing under our feet, and it is as if our old view of things has become obsolete. As we felt earlier in our careers, we again find ourselves looking at a future where we need to use our resourcefulness, adaptability, and creativity to find a great situation for ourselves.

The interesting thing is that no matter what causes the awakening, one day we all find ourselves at the mid-career crossroads. And what we do then can bring us a great deal of future satisfaction, though at the time it feels terrifying.

How To Know You're at the Mid-Career Crossroads?

1. You've been working between 25 and 35 years.

2. You worry about how you will live later in life and if you will need to do "this job" until you retire.

3. You have reached a fairly high level in your organization. The "mountains yet to climb" are fewer and harder to scale.

4. You wonder what would bring you great satisfaction for a long time, like you felt early in your career.

5. You feel like you don't know which way to turn, and your friends and colleagues don't seem to know how to help you.

Mastering the Crossroads

In order for this time to move from fear-inspiring to goal-directed, we need to realize that there are four main dynamics underlying the mid-career crossroads. These dynamics are interesting internal work that can help us reclaim our personal power as multi-faceted women. The four dynamics are to reduce our reliance on the opinions of others, acknowledge our fear about aging without letting it intimidate us, reduce external obligations to others, and get beyond the fear of having rusty skills.

Revisit the Importance of External Praise and Judgment by Others. It's very important to honor yet move past our tendency to feel worthy only when others say so. My experience and that of many clients is that we learn this reliance early in our careers, when we looked to external feedback from others to determine our success. Having important roles was a right we all fought for, and getting in to good jobs and proving ourselves became not only a skill, but a way of thinking about our lives.

Think of your own experience -- as a young woman entering the workplace, whose opinion mattered most? What kind of feedback did you really desire? Remember for a moment your sense of accomplishment when you were able to get things done efficiently, as well or better than the men who hired you, and when you were praised for your accomplishments. List 2–3 of the types of specific recognition you received in the chart below.

Recognition for Great Work Early in My Career

When & Where	What Happened?
1.	
2.	
3.	

Take a minute and think about this feedback. How is it similar or different than the kind of external recognition you pursue now, at this stage of your career? And how you're your need for this approval changed over time? For some of us, the feedback is different, but the need for approval is just as strong as when we were in our 20's.

Here's a secret – though these initial formative experiences were important at the time, at the crossroads we experience now, we logically realize that we no longer have so much to prove. We've "been there, done that" and are able to reset our decisions based on our desires and natural strengths. To the extent that inside, we're still looking for approval from the authority figures who say we are "good" and "smart", it's like we are two people at once—capable and skilled professionals, yet also more traditional women, wanting belonging and a sense that we are good enough.

This dichotomy inside ourselves is painful, and perhaps we push down the difference, preferring not to look at it. Or we alternate, depending on our internal self-confidence level on any given day. Or the most difficult, we evaluate ourselves based on the overall feedback from others that we get every day, so our fate is tied to how the client reacts, the boss nods or says no, or how our peers comment on us.

It's hard to escape these feelings—we accepted them as part of the "package" when we started work. But inside, we know that we need to transcend these feelings in order to move forward. Leaving the crossroads is a journey of self-worth and becoming the driver in our own career next steps.

Fear of Aging. Another aspect of the crossroads is the feeling of vulnerability based on looking older. No matter what age, we want to be attractive, vital, young, and accepted as interesting. Many women buy anti-aging creams, do Botox, or get Smartlipo or tucks in order to enhance their value to society and to postpone the day when they are less special - "just another person". At the crossroads, the fear of losing vitality is high, and the fear of competing (on looks alone) with younger women in the workplace can escalate as well.

Rather than deny this, it's important to reset our view of our worth in positive terms. After menopause (or the more socially correct term – in our 50's), the journey to find a new identity without losing our old exciting selves is a matter of trial and error, and can either be taxing or a super adventure. The number of books devoted to positive affirmations, meditation, and spirituality/graceful transition has grown tremendously and can really help us. But mostly, a love filled life where our internal worth is seen no matter what the mirror shows provides the best support for this necessary journey. Embracing new roles and finding time to spend with loved ones is not just a "nice to have" at the crossroads and beyond – it's essential to positive personal growth.

Reduce External Obligations. Many women today are the main breadwinners for their families and many also support their young adult children well into their 20s. The freedom to change jobs and de-stress, to do what we really would love to do, seems to evaporate like the morning dew.

How to categorize, prioritize, phase down, and release enough of these obligations to make a good choice for happiness and productivity in the second half of worklife takes courage and planning. Many times it seems unbearable to disappoint another who depends on us. Unfortunately, in sparing another, we disappoint ourselves. You really cannot avoid this choice. So the issue is to figure out a phased plan where those depending on your income see that there is a timeframe after which they will be on their own, or where you plan that your income will decrease but your availability will increase. You may not be in this situation, but if you are, please realize that it's entirely possible to find ways to break free a bit from what feels like the multitude of tiny strings which together trap the giant in "Gulliver's Travels".

Get Past Worrying that Skills are Rusty. For many at the crossroads, we realize that we have been promoted to a leadership job that we would like to leave (step back from, so to speak). But, depending on how long we have been away from the line work, we worry that our current skill level is a bit too rusty for any real change. Facing this fact and doing something about it seem too tough while we are working all day in our current position. So a better way to deal with the crossroads is to harvest natural skills we already have, determining those we just need to renew vs. learn from scratch.

Summary and Learning Points

In summary, at the Crossroads, just as in our late 20s, we feel the call for something more in life. Many of us once answered this through a family, marriage, or big job. In our mid-career, we also feel that pull to another stage of life. There are a few differences, of course. But bottom line, the risk we faced in our 20s is no smaller than the one we face now. We were terrified then, and we can be terrified now. The difference is that when we started out, we just went for it. Now, it seems like we can't afford to make a mistake.

Successfully navigating mid-career means that we find a way to see that no matter what we do, we will learn and grow and it will be ok. We need to move forward anyway, using as much information as we can. Since things are always changing, we won't see every risk or opportunity. Even though the future is never completely predictable, making the decision to move to another way of working, if you want to do that, is smart, and doing something is more important than making the "right" choice.

We all evaluate risk differently, and, of course, it's important that we take actions that fit our style from a risk standpoint. Like with any journey, it takes planning, decision-making, timing, good fortune, and capability.

So, as you can see, the journey at the "Crossroads" at mid-career is mainly an "inside journey" within your own mind, emotions and spirit. I think we avoid the conclusions of this journey because we only see what we might have to give up, not the price we are paying by remaining in something too long. Because this is the first place many women get stuck, we'll spend some time on untangling the emotions and coming to logical conclusions.

So let's figure out how to get ourselves moving. There are three main tasks:

Three Actions to Move Past the Crossroads	
Action 1	Reset your career view
Action 2	Acknowledge need for new plan
Action 3	Commit to use your insights

Action 1: Reset Your Career View – Consider how much you think you have "at stake" in your current situation and whether you feel you need to keep up the same pace and work for the foreseeable future. Just thinking about this, you may realize that you don't want to keep the same pace but

you cannot see how to stay important if you slow down your hours.

It's hard, but important, for all of us in mid-career to find ways to begin to let go of those assumptions about what makes us important, and to rethink what the ideal schedule would be for your interests, skills and energy level.

Try this for a minute. Think about letting go of your title. You are no longer the Chief Administrative Officer, the Regional Field Manager, the partner in the law firm, the COO, or whatever your title is now. Feel the freedom that letting go of your "title" brings. And feel the loss you would have if you did give it up. What would you lose? Colleagues, status, midnight emails, 24/7 even on vacation, self-importance, some politics, and maybe some money (but not necessarily).

I'm not here to tell you what to do, but even if you stay in your current role for a while longer, eventually (before you are 60) it's absolutely necessary to reclaim your control of your worklife because there are few role models for any "standard" path, except waiting to retire. Resetting your career view helps you to broaden your future options.

A Story to Help Broaden our Thinking

Imagine yourself on a beautiful highway just at dawn, in springtime. The light is gorgeous and the air is soft. You feel peaceful and energized for the journey ahead and are attracted by the great place you are headed to. You are not anxious or stressed, physically, mentally, emotionally, or spiritually. You feel alive, like you are meant to take this trip, that it will be an important and positive opportunity in your life.

This is what careers are supposed to feel like. The root of career is "calling," a sense of purpose and meaning attached to work. If in the mind's eye of the journey described above, you felt yourself as the driver of a vehicle, you would have the choice to slow down, enjoy the moment, take a rest, take a photo, or unexpectedly stop to explore a town along the way.

You could also easily speed up, trying to make a certain destination by nightfall. You could take a bigger freeway using your GPS or spend a lot of time in the passing lane. In the end where you get is the same, just faster. Or you could rethink your journey entirely and plan to cut it short or change destinations.

It is easy to picture the ideal of what careers could be. Usually the career highway is not the leisurely, lovely, light-filled highway at sunrise. More often, it is filled with a lot of the traffic of competition, the delays in progress from organizational change, the noise of the street as coworkers publicly praise and privately compete with each other.

Use the chart below to think through your views about your career to date. The chart will help you to reflect on the fears, goals, needs, and wants from your work, early in your career till now. Your answers will help you see what has changed internally and what has stayed the same over time. Use the chart below to mark importance levels. Mark "H" for "high importance," "M" for "moderate," and "L" for "low or not important." Then, write your insights in the space under the chart. We'll use it in the next section.

How my Views of Work have Changed Over Time

Fill in colums and use H-High, M=Medium, L-Low to mark

Fears about Work (H, M, L)	In my 20's	30 – 40's	40+
Having a bad boss			
Not getting a job			
Not being good enough			
Discrimination for age or gender			
Needs Met by Work	**In my 20's**	**30 – 40's**	**40+**
Security			
Belonging			
Achievement			
Appreciation			
Personal Value Fulfillment			
Wants in Life	**In my 20's**	**30 – 40's**	**40+**
Personal life balance			
Be remembered			
Be visible			
Youthfulness/vitality			
Have fun/adventure			
Good health			
Be attractive			

Life Goals	In my 20's	30 – 40's	40+
Be authentic			
Like yourself as is			
Choose your own path			
Leave guilt behind			
Have friends/good relationships			
Be comfortable			
Have free time			

What insights did you gain from thinking about your past? Notice which aspects have been important for your whole career, and which have changed in importance over time. Remember these insights – they will be important in your forward planning.

My Insights about Past Fears, Needs, Wants and Goals

Category	Insight	How I Plan to Use It
Fears		
Needs		
Wants		
Life Goals		

A second way to reset your career view is to identify how well you take positive action already to achieve your goals. In the simple quiz below, mark "yes" or "no" to each item, and then count the number of yes responses. Your answers will give you a sense of what you already do and what you will need to focus on to get yourself moving.

Career Action Self-Assessment

No.	My Career Action Self-Assessment	Yes/No
1.	I set career goals every year.	
2.	I look around to see what new opportunities there are.	
3.	I consciously stop doing tasks that are obsolete or that waste my time.	
4.	I am ready to match my natural skills and interests to my next job.	
5.	I make sure I get the raises I deserve.	
6.	I ensure that I don't give too much of my life to my job.	
7.	I have a "plan B" that I could put into action if something happened to this job.	
8.	When I am frustrated at work, I think about the possibility that I may have outgrown this situation.	
9.	I believe that each job has a life-cycle after which it is time to move on.	
10	If I leave, I will not feel like a quitter.	
11	I trust my ability to get another good work situation that is positive and pays well.	
12	I am not planning to retire, just slow the pace later.	

Scoring Your Answers

If you had 10 or more "yes" responses, you are proactive and ready internally to make a move. Seven to nine "yes" responses means you have some work to do but generally take responsibility for your future work. Six or fewer "yes" responses means that you have granted others the ability to determine your fate. Whatever your score, think about the opportunities you have to really reset things to match your internal spirit and talents going forward.

How was it to answer these questions? Did you feel the pull to say you were more active than you really are? It's okay, many of us have that same "superwoman" idea rolling around in our heads. But from a logical standpoint, all 12 items are important for a fully functioning career, especially one where you will need to stand up for yourself and go outside of your comfort zone.

Making Great Decisions – Left, Right, Back, or Forward

Here's a third way to reset your career view and to remember to trust your own judgment. Give yourself a minute to list 3–4 of the great decisions of your life. These include decisions that worked out to result in some of the best aspects of your life but also decisions that turned out badly at the time but led to a period of growth.

Examples: You chose the right school to maximize your personal growth. You chose a good job to learn a craft.

Great Decisions of My Life		
What I Decided	What Resulted	How It Strengthened Me

Remembering these great decisions and that you took a risk or sacrificed a bit to implement your decision should help you to reset your career view and to become confident in your judgments about what kind of change would work best for you now.

Action 2: Acknowledge It's Time for a New Plan – Looking at what you wrote above, you may be thinking that it's pretty logical that you are a smart, talented woman who has accomplished a lot and makes good, even great decisions. Yet many women I have helped find themselves emotionally vulnerable. As we discussed earlier, these feelings are normal at this time of your career. So in order to get yourself moving again, look back at one of the decisions you made earlier that was pretty risky and didn't even work out that well at the time, and look for the positive lesson from that. Here's a personal example that many people have – a move to another state for work or personal circumstances:

Money Isn't Everything...

After ten years of living in Hawaii, a job change for my first husband led to a decision to move to Seattle. Logically it made sense because the economy was terrific there, jobs were plentiful and it seemed prosperity was easier to find. However, less than a year later, our family returned to Hawaii, less prosperous and completely stressed. For a while I counted that move as a failure. But later I realized that I had learned something important about life that I wouldn't likely have learned any other real way – that is, that prosperity is not measured in dollars alone. Having read this statement - that money can't buy happiness - my whole life, it hadn't sunk in at all until I experienced it myself.

By acknowledging that even risky decisions worked out, you help to reduce your fear of trying something new again. In The Change Cycle™, a great change management tool that I am fortunate to be a master trainer for, they describe this as discerning the real fears from the unreal fears. However you describe it, realizing that you can learn and prosper from every decision is an important feeling to propel you forward.

So, what's your story? And how does it show you that your decision to make a change can be beneficial no matter how it looks from the outside?

My BEST "Worst" Decision	
What happened:	
What I learned:	

Action 3: Commit To Use Your Insights – Make an agreement with yourself that fear is better than regret, and know that pushing through the fear is something you have done before and can do again. One easy way to get yourself to action is to recall how you have gone through anxious times in the past and moved yourself even though you were afraid. This could be when you took your last job, when your child left home for the first time, when you had to confront someone close to you with tough news, or when you had a health challenge.

Whatever it was, use the short reflection below to bring it to mind. Once you do, promise yourself that you will use that method plus be open to new ones to get yourself moving forward again.

My Agreement To Push Past Fear

What kinds of fears typically hold me back:

How I have pushed through these fears in the past:

What I commit to myself now:

PART 2:
Your Past – Looking Back to Move Forward

In women's lives, careers have taken a strong near-equal place beside family, leisure time, and community service, sometimes even taking over first place. We have chosen this path (mostly) and have thrived from the feelings of accomplishment, professional growth, and prosperity that we derive from our jobs and careers.

We, along with everyone who takes the career journey, have labored in the early stages to find our way, prove our worth, master the skills and job, and challenge ourselves once again with even "higher mountains." Think back to all the jobs you had, to the challenges you overcame. You paid your dues.

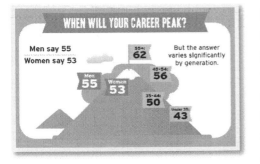

For women, in a different way than men, we have found the on-ramp to career success far easier to navigate than the exit ramp, detour, or alternate route. It seems that we didn't realize we would have a hard time leaving, once we got to "have it all."

Many women I've talked to speak about the difficulty in getting their spouses, friends, colleagues, and even their children to support alternative career choices once they have "made it." Wondering why that is, I researched it and found that we have become trapped in the obligations loop that men found themselves in—that is, we became part of the family "success story," the breadwinner who helped the family to prosper.

For women, who (at least many of us) felt we were self-expressing but not "holding down the fort" for our families, this awareness has been alarming and, for some, debilitating from a career-change standpoint. We end up bored, distracted, and feeling like a commodity, stale and stuck, and we think that we will just "stick it out" until someone rescues us with a new (bigger) job offer or until we hopefully retire.

Why Mid-Career Is Our Time To Break Out

Whether you think you are at your peak yet or not, it's important to think about what you will do once you have reached that peak. Mid- to late career is a really special time for a career change and is different than what you have experienced up to this point. Now you have a track record of different jobs, and you have an idea of what you like and don't like. At this point, if you are looking for something completely new, it's tough to tell if the feelings you have are because you're burned out, just tired, or that you actually do need something new.

It's also kind of hard to sort out the difference between your physical changes in midlife and what's going on at work. Most of us don't feel comfortable talking about this facet with almost anybody, even our spouse, because it makes us feel vulnerable.

This section shows you how to use the information about your past jobs and feelings to tell what's really going on now and also to give you a marker for which way to go in the future. Logically, we know that it's about time that we altered our path a bit instead of doing what we've always done. If we are bored now, to just replace it with another job that's similar will lead to similar results. It's like driving around in a circle.

It's important to open ourselves up to all possibilities, including lateral moves, part-time work, or even moving backwards for a while in order to build new confidence and experiences in life. The first step in using the information we collected so far is to look back and ask ourselves the question, "What kind of paths have I enjoyed the most so far?"

There are several paths, some traditional and others more specialized and unique. The more you have experienced, the more easily you can choose new options at this midpoint in your journey.

So, it's time to look back. Careers and jobs are vehicles for your self-expression in the world. Here, you will look back to learn from yourself. If you are highly analytical, you can also take additional surveys and reflection. You'll look back in two ways:

1. First, you'll look back to your past jobs, their highs and lows, to extract the important difference between your best and worst jobs and to consider how that assessment compares with your current role. The review will help you realize what you want to seek and never want to do again.

2. You'll determine what characteristics you want to keep in your future jobs. These characteristics include type of work, pay, schedule, and type of structure, including boss, size of company, or solo work.

Types of Career Pathways – Your Rearview Mirror

Take a look at the following table about the major types of careers. Pick the one or two that you have followed so far.

Career Pathways

Path	Description	Success Equals	Advantages
Traditional	Promotion and higher responsibility —working through others. Move out of professional and into generalist.	Status, authority, money, level.	Well understood by society.
Professional	Professions with clear "career ladder," such as sales, marketing, human resources, law, medicine, engineering, teaching, clergy, etc.	Keep moving along the path of systematic advancement within the profession.	Status, authority, expert in field. Professional respect.

Lifelong Sequence of Jobs, Not a "Career"	No value judgment is made about the worth of position or direction of movement. Can go in and out of organizations if need be.	Learn something from each job. Use similar skills from one job to another.	Flexible, less restrictive Works well in times of change or for second career.

Which have you followed? By looking at the path you chose vs. the ones you didn't, it helps in two ways. First, you can see in the path you chose how you likely view success, and if you choose a change you may need to detach yourself from some of the advantages to make a change. Second, it shows you that whatever path you chose is not the only one. That insight is very useful.

Now that you have looked at the general path you have chosen, let's get more specific. Looking back at the jobs comprising your career is extremely powerful and can allow you two important abilities. First, you will realize just how many situations you have experienced successfully in whatever career you have had. Just remember that there should be no judgment by you about whether there were "too few" or "too many" regrets. Just look at the patterns of joy and fulfillment that can take you forward once again. Secondly, you will see what your personal pattern has been and which aspects have matched you vs. been a miss in various jobs.

Here's an example from Jessica, who, at 45, was looking for something new but was confused. As you look at her "rearview mirror" career map, look for trends that would help her decide what to pursue and avoid in her next jobs. Remember, this is prior to adding in her personality and life values.

Jessica's Career Journey (Highs and Lows) So Far

Job 1	My Summary
Sales Associate in Retail, at 22 years old, for 3 years	I did it to get my foot in the door in sales. It was a big company and I thought I would start in one job and move up eventually.
	I liked it because I am naturally outgoing and have a good memory, so I could learn the product easily. I don't take things personally so wasn't upset if I was rejected on any cold calls.
	The money was ok, enough to survive, but with a lot riding on commission, there were months where I really wondered what would happen with bills.
	There was little status, we were considered replaceable and were told that often.
	My boss yelled a lot, but I learned from him. The stress was mostly in turning in paperwork. I really don't like that but it was necessary to get my commission.

The most fun was watching experienced sales people get things done, and testing myself to get better. I really loved meeting new people.

Overall I'd give this job a 5 on a 1-10 scale. I hated the hours and the boss just never lightened up.

Job 2	My Summary
Marketing Manager for Small Advertising Firm, at 26 years old for 4 years	I had finished my B.A. in Sales and Marketing and took this for a real professional job and to have a better pay plan and security than a regular sales path. I thought there would be more status and better hours and regular pay.

I had to write marketing and PR pieces and I liked that because I write well and am creative. But my boss was not creative and didn't really "get" where my work was coming from. It was a source of stress because he would evaluate my work – I always wondered how he got into this department.

The money was ok but not great. And the job had a nice title but no real status. I was stressed about deadlines and lack of clarity about what my boss wanted.

I worked 45-50 hours on the phone and at my desk.

One of my coworkers, Sally, was a good mentor and that was terrific. I guess I learned in this job that your boss is not always right, but you have to navigate that anyway.

The most fun was the thrill of taking on a new piece and seeing what I could do with it.

Overall I'd give this job a 6 on a 1-10 scale, because of my mentor and my security level.

Job 3	My Summary
Sales Manager at a local Advertising Company **At 32 years old for 10 years (after a break for 2 children)**	I did it to get back in to work. It was the first job offered once I started searching. I was a manager really for the first time. I found that I was good at teaching and getting people to work well. I guess I learned what not to do from my other bosses. I was able to set realistic targets and to deal with customers. My senior manager had a different style from me – was more of a disciplinarian, but I didn't have trouble with him. I just made sure my people weren't hurt by his style. The money was good and there were bonuses. I liked this a lot. I woked 60+ hours per week and this was hard on my family. I learned that status has a price. I rate this job a 7 out of 10. I liked my people, the job, the money and status, and I would have stayed if I didn't relocate.

Job 4 – My current Job	My Summary
Copywriter – working remote for a company in another state, At 42 years old, have been doing it for 3 years	My husband got a job in another state and we relocated. I wanted some flexibility to help my children adjust, and the security of regular work. I am pretty much alone most of the time and that takes getting used to. I miss being with people. But I found that I can make pretty good relationships remotely, and I am disciplined enough to work this way. I get to use my creative and writing skills. It's just that there are too many assignments at once – like I am the dumping ground for whatever cannot get done in the actual office. The pay is fair – I am paid on a salary vs. by the word or project. For my family this is the best arrangement – otherwise I would be working all the time. The tasks are clear and my boss is supportive. We talk every few hours by phone or Skype. I rate this job a 3 out of 10. Being alone and having all this pressure just isn't for me. I need to be in a group where we can connect and share ideas, and where I feel a part of a real team.

What did you notice as you read through Jessica's list?

Here are some obvious things:

- Jessica kind of "fell into" her first job, as many of us do.
- She thought promotion was a good career path and found out that the particular circumstances matter a lot.
- She had to leave the workforce for a time and then find a way back in.
- She had one good job (sales manager) and though she liked her team, she didn't do well with the style difference with her own manager.
- Money has not been particularly plentiful, except in one job, and seems more important to her than she lets on.
- Working completely remotely is not a good match for Jessica.

Before we leave Jessica, what advice would you give her for options she could pursue in her next 2–3 jobs?

Advice for Jessica

Things to pursue:

Things to avoid:

Now, it's your turn! Use the chart or think about it the way Jessica did, adding jobs and categories that match you.

My Job History –
Trends and What They Tell Me

Description	Describe and rate three jobs you have had		
	Job	Job	Job
1. My Age			
2. Number of Years			
3. Why I did it?			
4. Skills I Used and Learned			
5. Stresses I had to Deal With			
6. How was the Money?			
7. What Kind of Status Did I Have?			
8. What Hours, Schedule, Workload?			
9. How Supportive Were Boss and Peers?			
10. What was interesting?			
On a 1-10 Scale with 10 being Best Ever!, Rate this Job			

What insights did you get from your own past jobs review? If you are like most people, it is enlightening and also possibly a bit sad, as you realize that there were times you knew it was time to leave, but you didn't. Don't dwell on this aspect – you know, it happens to almost everyone at least once. But learn from it, and focus on what you saw from past jobs that worked well and that you want to pursue in the future.

As you look back for insights, try to surface your definition of what constituted success for you at that time. This part of looking back is intended to free you up to make a new choice in the future. At this time, it's important to rethink job satisfaction and redefine the criteria you use to evaluate it. How important, now and in the future, is the same amount of money, prestige, the chance to use your skills, and work you enjoy? And, how are these features different for you now, from earlier phases of your worklife?

Commit to use your insights in the space below.

Things to Pursue

Things to Avoid

How I think my future success definition is different from my past

PART 3: The Present –
How Your Current Job Stacks Up

Looking at your answers about what to pursue and avoid, honestly assess your current job. In the space below, list those things that your current job offers and where it falls short.

How My Current Job Stacks Up

What my current job offers that I would like to repeat:

Where my current job falls short:

.

PART 4: Summary and Decide – Time for a New Journey

This part has the fewest words, but the biggest impact! Reflect for a moment and create a clear message to yourself about what general direction will make you happy in your next few jobs. The crossroads you faced are actually a compass, and this compass shows direction from where you are today. Don't worry about being correct – you can draft something now and review it again later to refine it.

What Will Make Me Happy in Future Jobs:

Describe in 1-2 sentences your insights about future direction, based on the reflection you have done.

In the future, I want ....

Summary - Roadblocks and Accelerators

As you move out of this phase and into your new career roadmap, a few things can get in your way, and others can propel you forward. I've called them roadblocks and accelerators. Your job is to avoid or acknowledge the roadblocks without getting stuck, and actively seek out the accelerators. For Phase 1, here are your most likely roadblocks and accelerators.

Roadblocks:

- Minimizing the validity of your own experience. Doubting your inner voice.
- Settling and thinking you don't deserve more.
- Refusing to give anything up about the situation you already know.
- Being afraid to discuss the situation with your partner or family.

Accelerators:

- Comparing this time to when you first started out and were willing to try new things without proof they would work.
- Finding another woman who made a successful career change and asking her questions about how she did it.
- Finding a career coach.

Phase 2:
Create Your
Mid-Career Roadmap

	PART 1: Your Unique Style
	<ul><li>Your Personality and Ideal Work</li><li>Your Natural Skills and Talents</li><li>Your MPG – Meaning, Prosperity, and Growth</li></ul>
Phase 2 – Create Your Mid-Career Roadmap	**PART 2:** Pull It All Together
	<ul><li>Your Preferred Routes – How to decide</li><li>Your Turn – Summarize your unique style and preferred routes</li><li>Roadmap Research</li></ul>
	Roadblocks and Accelerators

From Phase 1, you can see that preparing to make a change can be challenging but satisfying. Rethinking our life's work patterns can be unsettling, and yet many of us have had the experience where our most unsettled times have led to fun and prosperity once we embraced the change. And for many professional women, to embrace the change means that we need to have a plan that we think fits us and that protects us from failure, as well as is one we can explain to those close to us.

Yes, most of us have a general nagging feeling that we should do things in our working life that we like, are good at, and that naturally draw us. But most of us, except the most ambitious, don't actually have a specific plan that we compare our reality against. Rather, many of us think generally about leaving a job for something better, and then somehow time passes, things change, and we wait and complain. Or even worse, if things become even less positive than before, we blame ourselves because we didn't trust our intuition.

In order to get out of this trap, it is essential to evaluate the job situation in an analytical, neutral way. If we don't, from a whole life fulfillment perspective, we are making a potentially costly decision. In Marcus Buckingham's book, *Go Put Your Strengths To Work*, he notes that only 17% of people say that they are able to use their biggest strengths,[2] MOST of the time, at work. That's a pretty depressing statistic.

---

[2] Marcus Buckingham, Go Put your Strengths to Work: 6 Powerful Steps to Achieve Outstanding Performance (New York: Free Press, 2011)

Yet, it's predictable that many people would not find a strengths match at work. Many of us "fell into" our careers, and stayed in the field of the first job we got. Many people seek security over fulfillment, at least in the first part of their careers, and over time come to think that they cannot have both. So using personal talents and strengths goes to the bottom of the priority list, and doing what one is asked stays at the top.

As a result, many people who could do better from a personal fulfillment standpoint stay in jobs they aren't well suited for. They take negative feedback, and try to change, even if what they are being asked to do does not fit their strengths. The assumption is that in a traditional career path, anything that does not match what the organization needs is a personal weakness. That is, over time we may become conditioned to think that we are not good enough just the way we are.

We think that other jobs in other places may result in the same problems that we have currently. And although there is a small chance that is true, the likelihood is that if we were clear on what would match us the best, other situations would better fit us and we would be happier, better able to use our natural strengths, and feel valuable and fulfilled in that work. We only have one life to live, as far as we know. So we need a way to figure out which options would really work best for us.

Matching future work to our natural selves includes two parts, 1) Your Unique Style, which includes your personality, ideal work settings, your natural talents, and your MPG™ -

Meaning, Prosperity and Growth. Clarifying your unique style is easier than you might think. If you are analytical and like detailed thinking, you can go deeply into the process. For others, who like quicker decisions or who have thought about some of this recently, it can be as simple as "learning from yourself" – just a matter of thinking back to when you have been the happiest and why. Taking this relatively brief amount of time to write down the "match" will be one of the most powerful things you can do to really achieve personal career fulfillment going forward. It's not an "exercise." It's validating yourself, using supporting data where it makes sense.

2) The second part is to find "Your Preferred Route". Included in your preferred route are the functional types of work you wish to do that use your talents, your preferred length of time in each job, and the amount of money you want to make ideally. Each aspect will be evaluated separately. Please use the chart below to summarize your results, so that you can see it everything in one place. The chart will be repeated at the end of this phase in a roadmap format as well, to prepare for the next phase, "Use your Roadmap".

My Unique Style
and Preferred Route

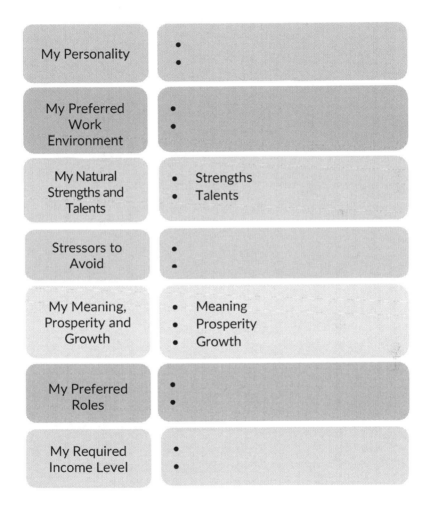

| My Personality | • |
| | • |

| My Preferred Work Environment | • |
| | • |

| My Natural Strengths and Talents | • Strengths |
| | • Talents |

| Stressors to Avoid | • |
| | • |

My Meaning, Prosperity and Growth	• Meaning
	• Prosperity
	• Growth

| My Preferred Roles | • |
| | • |

| My Required Income Level | • |
| | • |

PART 1:
Your Unique Style

What is your style? It is the collection of personal qualities that uniquely and specifically describe what you will love to do, how you will want to do it, and what kind of setting and conditions will work best for your. Your style is linked to your "things to pursue" from Phase 1, but because your style is more specifically measureable, it is easier to take action on.

Listed below are the aspects we will look at.

- Your Personality
- Your Ideal Work Environment
- Your Natural Skills and Talents
- Your Meaning, Prosperity, and Growth

Your Personality and Job Match

When people make a change in their careers, why don't they think about matching it to their personalities? I guess some think that personality is a fixed thing and that people should adapt to whatever the job requires. As I mentioned, early in our careers, that makes sense because we're paying our dues and fitting into someone else's model of what we should do with our lives. But when we arrive at 45 or 50 years old and realize we have accomplished a lot of things and adapted to what people want from us for a couple of decades or more, it's time for us to think differently.

Similar to the "Strengths Finder" where you find ways to use your natural strengths at work, a personality match takes your normal traits and helps you put them into the planning process for your next few jobs.

Many of you have probably taken a personality assessment sometime in your career, especially if you've been in the corporate world. The main personality assessments used today are the Myers-Briggs (MBTI), the DiSC assessment, the Five Factors, and the Birkman assessment. In my practice, I've used three of these four assessments, and I can honestly say that each one of them measures different aspects, but they're all valuable, so I would encourage you to look back at your results to see any insights about what you need in a job, so that you don't have to always adapt beyond your comfort zone.

I'm currently using the Birkman in my work, and that instrument is very useful for careers for number of reasons, one being that it predicts the ideal work environment and also links to the *Dictionary of Occupational Titles*. A major advantage is that it combines both career and interpersonal strengths in one easy assessment. Based on your own responses, it tells you which careers your responses match with successful people already working in those jobs. For example, even though you may be an architect, accountant, lawyer, or politician, you could have the ability to be successful as a distribution warehouse supervisor, writer, political scientist, advocate for a cause, or the leader of a not-for-profit organization. If you wish to take the Birkman Assessment[3] to get a comprehensive career report, please contact a certified consultant. Besides myself, there are over 2000 worldwide. Or you can check out the excellent book *The Birkman Method: Your Personality at Work*, by Sharon Birkman Fink.[3]

In case you don't want to take a new assessment or drag out your old results, you can get a quick approximation of several key factors by using the quiz below. This personality quiz doesn't require you to answer many questions. It simply asks to choose from one of two adjectives in each row, and mark the center column, so you create a profile line down the center.

---

[3] The Birkman Method is a Trademark and registered Service Mark, and is used with permission.

My Personality at Work

Outgoing	Mark the dot that matches YOU best	Quiet
Love being with people	● ● ● ● ● ● ● ●	Prefer to work alone
Like to be busy	● ● ● ● ● ● ● ●	Prefer to do things 1 at a time
Thick-skinned	● ● ● ● ● ● ● ●	Sensitive
Adventuresome	● ● ● ● ● ● ● ●	Cautious
Talk a lot	● ● ● ● ● ● ● ●	Prefer to listen
Like surprises, flexible	● ● ● ● ● ● ● ●	Prefer advance warning
Like to direct decisions	● ● ● ● ● ● ● ●	Like to collaborate
Relationship builder	● ● ● ● ● ● ● ●	Logical/task-focused

Once you have drawn your profile line, think about how your current and past jobs have met your natural personality. Make a note comparing your ideal type of schedule and work setting to what you saw in this quick quiz.

What Matches Me Best

My past jobs that matched my personality best:

My past jobs that did not match me well:

How my current job matches my personality:

The table below shows for reference a subset of the kinds of jobs which match various aspects of the personality quiz. Of course, these are just "food for thought" because there are complexities in personality that are not reflected here. And my contention is that the easiest start is to use skills you already have proven in your past jobs. So for now, just star* or circle any jobs which seem to match your personality.

Before you start, please note. It is fine if you stay in the same type of job or work. But here we are just looking at additional options to free up your thinking of what else you might do later.

My Personality Type	Types of Jobs
Outgoing	Sales, coordination, public media, speaker
Love being with people	Sales, internal position, SWAT team, or project team
Like to be busy	Operations Manager, troubleshooter
Adventuresome	Start-ups or businesses in growth mode
Talk a lot	Sales, membership, giving speeches, teaching, or mentoring
Like surprises, flexible	Project work
Relationship Builder	Networking coordinator, membership, vendor relations

Structured	Project management
Quiet	Jobs with clear structure where tasks are well-defined and success is clear
Prefer to work alone	Back office or work remotely
Prefer to do things 1 at a time	Flexible schedule with payment by milestones or deliverables.
Cautious	Back office functions, analysis, accounting, or QA
Prefer to listen	Coach, counselor, social services
Prefer advance warning	Routinized schedule such as temp agency where you can say yes or no
Logical/task-focused	Finance, operations, project management

Before you leave this section, go to the My Unique Style and Preferred Route chart and list which personality aspects and generally which types of jobs match your unique style.

Work Setting Characteristics

The next part of your unique style is your preferred work setting and characteristics. Choose the work setting characteristics that you prefer and that you would thrive in, based on your past experience or your strong calling. Only choose those that are "necessary," not "nice to have." Your list should be no longer than 6–8 items. Write them down on a sheet of paper.

MY WORK SETTING CHARACTERISTICS – Choose 6-8

High pay	Help a cause	Creative environment
Security	Help others	Low stress
Predictable work	Working with public	Self-improvement
Able to make decisions	Belonging to organization	Change and variety
Competition	Friendships at work	Precision and accuracy
Collaboration	Influencing people	Fast pace
High energy situation	Selling ideas, products	Recognition
Working under pressure	Working by myself	Exciting work
Meeting deadlines	Working through others (managing)	Clear rules and procedures
Solving problems	Be known for my expertise or knowledge	High standards
Solving crises	Make decisions	Flexible schedule
Status	Power and authority	Financial rewards
Quiet	Lot to do	Independence
Work outdoors	Physical challenge	Lifestyle match
Good benefits	Able to come and go	Active in community
Travel	Desk job	Friendly environment
Other		

List these on the wheel at the start of this phase, along with the income and other job match indicators.

As you look at your ideal match, what insights come to mind? How similar is where you want to go to where you have been? What is the biggest difference?

Work Setting Characteristics that Match Me

My best work setting characteristics:

Where have I had these before?

Which are most important going forward?

Other Insights:

And as you have seen where things have not matched you in the past, there is another important aspect of working environment to consider, and that is how to minimize unwanted stress. Here's an example:

Jennifer's Story

Jennifer worked as a nursing supervisor in a large urban hospital. She had great skills as a nurse and worked her way up to supervisor about 10 years ago. She was happy with the work, enjoyed teaching others and liked the schedule, pay and commute. But her personality was a perfectionist and she was sensitive to criticism, largely because she worked very hard at accuracy. So by the time anyone criticized her, she had already done so herself. About a year ago, the hospital administrator, her direct boss who was not a micromanager, left and was replaced by a new person who was very judgmental and criticized Jennifer and others frequently, to assure quality. Jennifer's worklife went from satisfied to high stress. But because of her perfectionist tendencies, and even though Jennifer was completely competent, she blamed herself and worked harder and harder to please, to no avail. It wasn't until Jennifer found a career coach that she realized that the job conditions no longer matched her unique personality.

What about you? What stresses you out at work? Make your list here:

My TOP FIVE Stressors at Work

Stressful Aspects of My Work	How it Links to My Personality
1.	
2.	
3.	
4.	
5.	

Jennifer's story shows us the trap of working harder and harder to be viewed as "good enough". Your stressors may not be the same as hers. But as you think about what does stress you, even if it is something unrelated to people, such as a long commute each day, realize that every stress reduces our sense of connection to our work. And the connection to work is very important to pursue as we move past mid-career.

It's hard to say but true – we only have a few more jobs to go! Let's make them the best they can be for who we already are. Even if you have been in a good situation and then when things change you want it to still work out, if after a change in structure, workload or people at a job, if you do not easily adjust within six months, start looking for a transfer or new job. Believe me, it won't get better on its own by your continued attempts to "fit" the new situation. While this is on your mind, make a note on your Unique Style Wheel in the Section titled "Stressors to Avoid".

Your Natural Skills and Talents

Ensuring a personality match for your work is essential because it allows you to thrive emotionally and reduce stress. Equally important, you need to match your natural strengths and talents with your work. Of course, you may be a person who loves to learn new things and to challenge yourself, so matching does not prevent that. But what it does is to put you in charge of the kinds of things you choose to learn.

For example, a woman, let's call her Emma, is a great technical writer, but as part of her current job she is expected to do administrative, repetitive tasks as well. Although she can do it, this part is difficult for her, and she procrastinates as a result. Certainly administration is not a natural strength for her. As long as it is less than 10% of her job, things are fine. But Emma was in an organization where "generalist" skills were becoming more valued. As a result, each year, the administrative portion became a larger percent, until finally Emma realized that the things she was naturally good at were less than half of her weekly activities. The best decision she made was to leave the job and find something closer to her natural talent.

Like Emma, your job may also match some aspects of your personality and your natural gifts, but you may also be told of the need to upgrade your skills or learn things you are not naturally gifted at. If you are like Emma, you put up with this for several years—you may feel like you have to because you are worried that you are being a quitter, a fraud, or being selfish; or you may feel that everyone has things they don't like about their work. Or you think things will change and the situation will improve. It doesn't happen and here's why.

We're taught to put up with the things that don't match us by the way businesses are structured. The performance review system requires people to improve in some areas that your boss perceives as weak. This is the way companies get work done—by making people adapt to job requirements that change over time. Because everyone has to be reviewed, for anyone who needs to improve, the boss is telling them that in a way they are flawed because the job needs something they cannot give.

Well, I'm here to tell you after a lifetime in human resources and a lifetime of coaching professionally, that we are not actually flawed, but none of us ever has a perfect job that remains that way forever, because business needs change and the easiest thing is to ask current employees to adapt. As a result, many of us work to improve in areas we have little interest in, or try to become strong in areas that will never be strengths for us. In one way, the organization's needs make sense. It's too expensive to let people be whatever way they want to be. But in another way, if you know the match is no longer there, please don't settle for way less than you deserve. Simply put, after having performance reviews for 25 or 30 years, you have a choice— to choose a job that you will naturally succeed at without being asked to change, or to continue adapting.

Clarifying Your Natural Skills and Talents

So honoring your natural skills and talents really helps you see what other options you have. Natural talents are a combination of things you can do that others have found extremely valuable, and things that you can do "in your sleep" with ease and mastery, even if these things have never been visible to anyone in a job you have held.

As you create your mid-career roadmap, remember that you are focusing on things that you will be able to do to make a prosperous living as time goes by – for example, even if you at some point have some kind of a temporary disability or if you choose to work less hours. In other words, you are consciously shifting from what you "can do" to what you are "masterful" at doing.

You can always continue to expand your interests and learn brand new skills, but at mid-career, it is wise to make one option for work a "bridge" from one natural strength or skill to a new position. Take some time to contemplate this. In the space below, complete the table as best you can, based on past performance. What have you been told you are great at?

My Summary of Natural Skills and Talents

Others think I am great at ...	When I have Used this Talent

Clearly, using natural talents in a work setting you prefer that matches your natural personality is a pretty attractive proposition. Thinking of it now, a pattern should be emerging that indicates which directions are most fruitful for you. You should also have clarity on which types of situations you should run from at all costs and never experience again in the 20 or so years of work you have left.

An example of a natural talent is the ability to sell any idea or product with charisma and the ability to read the person, or emotional intelligence. Another example is the ability to keep key numbers in your head and to do math quickly without a calculator. Another is the ability to intuitively know when to connect with another person. Another is the ability to cut through complex ideas into easily understood actions.

The list below shows talents that are valued and evaluated in the workplaces of today. They do not include your technical knowledge, but the other aspects of work. Looking at the list, mark those that are "no-brainers" for you, that you can do almost effortlessly.

MY Natural Skills and Talents			
Skill / Talents	check	**Skill / Talents**	check
Accepting Change		Active in meeting	
Implementing new projects		Handle self professionally	
Understanding business		Develop rapport easily	
Being proactive		Positive body language	
Time management		Sensitive to other's needs	
Planning and organizing		Write technical reports	
Meeting deadlines		Scheduling	
Keeping commitments		Editing/proofreading	
Customer service		Computer software skills	
Living the values		Grammar and spelling	
Producing a high volume at work		Prioritize work	
Taking initiative		Multi-tasking, efficiency	
Written communications		Advise or coach	

Collaboration		Create presentations	
Getting along with others		Analyze data accurately	
Persuading others		Prepare recommendations	
Selling products or ideas		Facilitate a group	
Following directions		Coordinate people	
Supporting corporate directions		Handle details	
Interpreting financial statements		Develop goals/ action plans	
Self-development		Conflict management	
Technical knowledge on the job		Speak effectively	
Listen actively		Create new policy	
Follow through		Motivate others	
Public speaking		Develop others/teach	
Handle difficult customer		Take appropriate risks	
Get work done through others		Delegate / share work	

Perform mathematical computations		Assess costs	
Documentations		Negotiate	

To show how many options there are, I've adapted a table drawn from the *Dictionary of Occupational Titles* and from the great, new book from DK Publishers called *Careers: The Graphic Guide to Finding the Perfect Job for You* that shows the kinds of interests, work schedule, location, relative pay, and personality that matches some key jobs.[4] I've adapted the list of jobs to add a column on late career jobs, but this is just a start for your thinking.

---

[4] Allison Singer (Ed.),Careers: The Graphic Guide to Finding the Perfect Job for You, (New York: DK Publishing, 2015)

Sample Jobs

General Field and Required Skills	Sample Early Career Jobs	Optional Late Career Jobs
Engineering and Manufacturing – intellectual curiosity, systematic, disciplined, focus on results, dependability of product	Civil engineer Mechanical engineer Electrical engineer Chemical engineer	Urban planning LEED/ENVISION Teacher/mentor Technical consultant
Sales Marketing and Advertising – verbal communications, flexibility and negotiations, customer focus, organizational skills	Real estate agent Buyer Store manager	Real estate broker Buyer for midlife and older retail locations Internet marketing manager
Business Management – problem-solving, leadership, interpersonal skills, customer focus	Functional manager Customer service manager Officer or retail manager Project manager	Consultant/instructor for business in field of expertise
Finance – interpersonal skills, strong intellect, good memory, numbers, good business knowledge	Auditor Risk manager Bank manager Investment banker Investment analyst	Finance instructor Accountant Management consultant

General Field and Required Skills	Sample Early Career Jobs	Optional Late Career Jobs
	Accountant Economist	
Law and Politics – verbal and written skills, problem-solving, negotiations, sensitivity	Lawyer Paralegal Arbitrator Politician	Judge Mediator Politician
Media and Journalism – verbal and written skills, working with people, perseverance, flexibility, and ability to meet deadlines	Newspaper journalist Broadcast journalist Editor Copywriter Online journalist	Online journalist Editor or copywriter
Arts and Design – creative, self-discipline, numerical skills, communicating complex ideas, attention to detail	Interior designer Design engineer	Home office with small clients or subcontract to larger groups
Social Science and Teaching – listening, patience, empathy, tact, problem-solving, ability to stay calm.	Social worker Counselor Occupational therapist Elderly home care	Counselor Teacher

* This chart is adapted from *Careers, The Graphic Guide to Finding the Perfect Job for You* (2015), DK Publishing

I've listed jobs that I believe are easy to do from your home, part-time, or freelance on a project basis because it's my contention that although you may remain in "corporate, full-time jobs" for a while longer, at some point in time, perhaps at 62, 65, or 68, when you want to keep working, being a manager or leader potentially has too much baggage associated with it, including politics, imposing change on others, and requiring you to not only care for your own productivity but the productivity of your team.

Contrast that, for example, with a mentor, copywriter, accountant, consultant, or other business advisor. These professions can basically work from anywhere and bring variety and a reduction in rules and structure, all the while requiring self-discipline and the ability to work alone.

Take a look at the chart and see if any of the "late career" options sound like they are worth investigating.

Summary

Looking back at this section, list the types of skills and talents that you could use in any new job to add value easily because of your level of skill or your natural talent. Then transfer the information to the wheel reprinted below from the beginning of this section.

My Unique Style
and Preferred Route

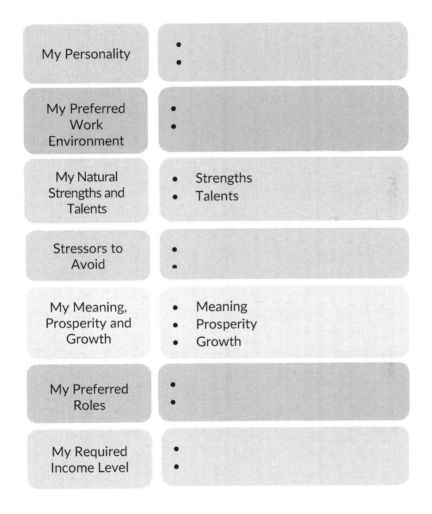

My Personality	• •
My Preferred Work Environment	• •
My Natural Strengths and Talents	• Strengths • Talents
Stressors to Avoid	• •
My Meaning, Prosperity and Growth	• Meaning • Prosperity • Growth
My Preferred Roles	• •
My Required Income Level	• •

Your MPG –
Meaning, Prosperity, and Growth

What gives you the most meaning out of work? What prosperity level do you need for the foreseeable future? What kind of personal growth and development do you want from your work? These three questions are pivotal to the direction and specific goals you will set for future jobs. Mid-career is the perfect time to review these and update them. You will define meaning by values and interests, define prosperity by your desired level of money and stress-reduced work, and growth by using the natural talents that you enjoy. Once you're done, you will use the insights to set your roadmap going forward.

MPG is an apt analogy to miles per gallon and to the fact that in any given pathway, you have a choice. It's up to you what mileage and success look like, and it can be different than what you once wanted.

As you identify what you actually want, be aware that granting yourself permission to create space to get these things is your biggest task. At the beginning, you may feel like you are never going to really find a job that matches your personality and skills.

Though no job is perfect forever, as you know, setting goals is the only way to consciously influence what happens to you. And, if you don't step back and set your own path, if you don't honor your own meaning and growth, you could stay in a job until it's too late and someone says it's time to go, or worse, you're obsolete. None of us deserve that fate. Women professionals growing up in the 70s have worked so hard for so long—it's time to claim the right to choose.

To define your current sense of *meaning, prosperity,* and *growth,* begin by thinking of your ideal job. What kind of accomplishments would you feel proud of? What kind of money and benefits would you have? What would stretch you, keeping you young and vital?

Meaning

Let's look at "meaning" at a bit deeper level. What constitutes meaning for you in your work? Is it freedom? Variety? Dedication to work? A sense of dependability? Accuracy? The ability to influence other people? Doing good for the world? An effective way to measure meaning, it turns out, is to assess your current top personal values.

Your values help you confidently move forward into a new age of career and work because they are deep-seated characteristics that you treasure. They can predict your satisfaction with the work choices you make. In fact, my research has shown that without any other metric, the match of personal values to the organization's real values (not just what is on paper) can predict how long we stay and whether we want to leave.

Honoring your values and seeking settings that match them help you move forward without fear in your work at this stage in your life.

Below you will see a list of personal values. Of the 25 values listed, please star or circle the top 5 that mean a great deal to you and that you want to express in your work. Or, if you wish, you can click the link and take a free assessment on the Barrett Values website.

http://www.valuescentre.com/our-products/products-individuals/personal-values-assessment-pva

Personal Values –Star or Circle Your Top 5

Accountability

Achievement

Ambition

Balance (home/work)

Clarity

Commitment

Community involvement

Compassion

Competence

Conflict resolution

Continuous learning

Cooperation

Courage

Creativity

Dependability

Enthusiasm

Environmental awareness

Efficiency

Ethics

Excellence

Fairness

Family

Financial stability

Forgiveness

Friendships

Future generations

Generosity

Health

Honesty

Humility

Humor/fun

Independence

Integrity

Initiative

Intuition

Job security

Listening

Logic

Making a difference

Mission focus

Open communication

Openness

Perseverance

Personal fulfillment

Personal growth

Power

Quality

Respect

Responsibility

Risk-taking

Safety

Self-confidence

Self-discipline

Success

Trust

Vision

Wisdom

Now, note the top values that you want to maximize in your future work. Notice whether or not things have changed for you in terms of what brings meaning; for example, a young person who early in her career wanted to express accomplishment, dependability, and being smart, after 20 years of work changed, and now values independence, variety, and balance.

My Top 5 Personal Values

1.

2.

3.

4.

5.

You have accomplished a lot of things in your life and in the future, so tracking these values to job options is a conscious process that can really pay off.

Prosperity

The first part of prosperity is money. There are three important factors to consider about money: things change, insurance is important, and making sure to avoid the fixed income trap. Let's face it, existing without enough money is just that, an existence. It's not a comfortable, fulfilling life, unless of course you choose to enter a monastery or become ascetic. So many people at mid-career and beyond focus their work choices only on whether they have enough to fully retire that it makes them old before their time.

Not that money isn't important; of course it is. Depending on the website you visit, you need 40% to 60% of your pre-retirement annual income to have a comfortable lifestyle, not counting unexpected costs, such as deteriorating health. And given the statistics about the savings rate in the United States, less than 20% of us actually have enough saved to even approximate this for very long.

In fact, the most recent statistics show that more than 40% of baby boomers near eligibility for retirement have saved less than 25,000 dollars, and 60% less than 100,000 dollars. Unless you believe in the tooth fairy or incredibly high market returns, that amount of money, if you fully retire, will last you less than five years if, for example, Social Security continues to wither under the pressure of so many of us leaning on it to supplement our meager earnings.

For women professionals, even if they are on track for savings, there are worries about being financially safe later in life. It's a dilemma because they may have a really "good job" from other's perspectives, but inside, they have lost the sense of prosperity and meaning. They are bored or feel like they don't have a sense of peacefulness about them anymore. Many of them want to choose to leave corporations and move out into freelance work. But the decision to do so takes courage and pre-planning for income and insurance.

To handle planning for "whole life prosperity" well, money, time and lifestyle all need to be included. Your goal is to create your definition of personal prosperity now and predict it going forward under various scenarios. To get a handle on prosperity, you need to think about the next 20 years, and take the time to include specific number estimates to the extent possible.

Possible Scenarios	At Age: 45–50	Age: 50–59	Age: 60–67	Age: 67+
Scenario 1 Partner, no ongoing family obligations				
Scenario 2 No partner, no major family obligations				
Scenario 3 No partner, major family obligations				

In the chart above, list how much money you need annually in each scenario. If you are more analytical, you can use a budget planning software like at mint.com https://www.mint.com/

The most important aspect of this analysis is to reduce your reliance on making the same or more than the amount you are making now, so that you have some "degrees of freedom" in which to explore new options. For example, you may want to create a sideline business and go from full-time to 30 hours a week. Since part of that income is variable, not salary, you would want some flexibility over the first year or so until you build up the growth of the new work.

In the space below, list your current income, how much is needed for basics, and what could be left over for new career options.

My Minimum Income Analysis			
A. Current Monthly Income	B. Amount Needed for home, food, utilities, health care, other necessities	C. Amount used for grown children, luxuries, travel, etc.	A minus B. How much do I actually need to make?
$	$	$	$

Let's look at a second aspect of prosperity, and that is well-being: spiritually, mentally, and physically. We all know people who are financially comfortable but completely out of whack in other areas of life, either through a slavish devotion to money, or a schedule that eats them alive. What we have called work-life balance is really a valuation of how friends, outside activities, family, and a sense of being, not just doing, make life worthwhile.

List the things that you value beyond work in the space below.

Things I value beyond work	How I experience them currently
1.	
2.	
3.	
4.	

Growth

For growth, I mean growth as a person and increasing your capacity to really achieve what you want for your life. For a person like me, growth means always looking ahead at what's a new trend and seeking knowledge that's related to my work or just in general. Over time, we should all have professional growth goals. If you think of it like a beautiful, leafy tree with a trunk about two feet around, at the trunk is growth of the core capabilities and natural talents you have. On the branches is growth in skill or experience along a capability you already are using. At the top is the new growth or areas of new exploration. At mid-career, you will focus on growth wherever you want, but for the biggest satisfaction, choose growth along your natural talents.

How does this link to the earlier discussion of natural skills and talents? Well, if the natural skills and talents are the trunk of the tree, that is the core – new growth would be 10-20% per year of your effort at the most.

For me, growth in my profession means . . .

Now that you have looked at *meaning, prosperity*, and *growth*, complete a chart like the one below for yourself. Estimate if your current job is 100%, then what percentage is *meaning* vs. *prosperity* vs. *growth*? Then, set a goal for future jobs that re-weight these.

Example – Sally's Current and Future MPG Goals

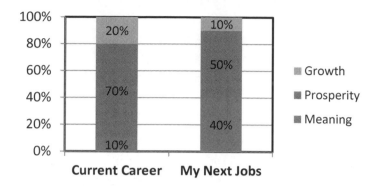

You can see in this example that in her current career, Sally is there mainly for the money and has only 10% from meaning and 20% in growth (which is imposed on her by her boss, not by choice). In her next jobs, she is setting a goal to increase her sense of meaning and what she is doing, to leave a legacy to 40%, keep income and prosperity at 50% (a slight reduction), and lower new growth to 10% (in other words, use her natural strengths more).

How would these charts look for you?

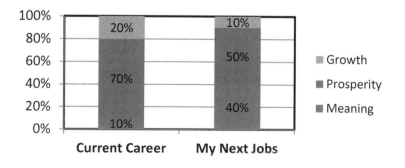

PART 2:
Pull It All Together

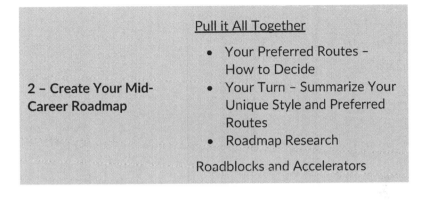

Pull it All Together

2 – Create Your Mid-
Career Roadmap

- Your Preferred Routes –
  How to Decide
- Your Turn – Summarize Your
  Unique Style and Preferred
  Routes
- Roadmap Research

Roadblocks and Accelerators

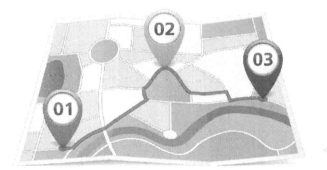

It's time to use the information you pulled together about your personal style to create the preferred routes for your personal roadmap. These routes are not something that you absolutely have to act on right away, but they are essential for high meaning and low stress in your life. It's your own directional plan, and it should be specific, even if you change it later. When you are finished, it should "feel" like the illustration above—organized and in some planned order.

At the beginning, though, it will likely feel more like this illustration—kind of messy, with more than one destination and route.

Although it may inspire in you some fear and second-guessing, this is normal and a sign that you are on the right track and should keep going forward. Staying in the "safe zone" of a job that has lost its luster is actually more risky than moving ahead from a "whole person" career standpoint. This is because the longer you stay in something that isn't working, the more you become obviously unhappy. And this unhappiness makes you less employable elsewhere.

So, use all that time you've invested in thinking and planning, and get ready to move forward!

Here are the questions that you should be able to answer by now:

- What increased sense of meaning or accomplishment would make it worthwhile for you to change jobs now or in the near future?
- What is the minimum level of income you will need from the new job or situation to pay your bills and be "safe" financially?
- What is the talent you strongly desire to use more often?
- What schedule and office/work setting are you looking for?
- What should a job location offer to match your natural personality?

So, assuming you are ready to create your roadmap, here's how to go about it.

"To pull it all together" means to take your current profession or any linked profession from your personality instrument, such as the Birkman Assessment, and determine which ways you could accomplish meaningful results in that profession that still match your personality, work settings, personal values, and financial and lifestyle preferences.

It may seem to you like a "mission impossible," but it isn't. Beyond my clients and countless other coaches, AARP's "Life Reimagined" website, Oprah's career website, and many others, our collective eyes are opening to the new possibilities for work beyond the all-encompassing, typical reality many of us have from 8 am to 7 pm, 6 days a week.

You can do it! You have all the knowledge you need. Let's use the data to prioritize possible paths.

Image – Pull It All Together

Imagine you are holding this steering wheel and you are going to turn it to move your career forward. As you prepare to do that, you notice all the arrows are pointing in and they represent all the insights you have collected about yourself, your talents, your job settings, and your financial needs. As you decide what your next best options are, you'll keep this multidimensional approach in mind—without letting it overwhelm you. Your goal is that it frees you to move ahead by giving you peace of mind that what you do next will actually fit you better than other positions you have held.

Of course, there is always some aspect of risk to every change, and this is no different.

But with internal knowledge, you can prevent mistakes that others have made by your proactive approach to determining options.

Sophie – Lessons Learned from the Traditional Path

Sophie was trained in systems and is a natural extrovert. She loves music and art, but hasn't had any opportunity to show it at work. She is a natural storyteller, often infusing her work with teaching moments. And for most of her career, she was a successful systems analyst who remained in specialty roles, working in retail, health care, and non-profit jobs in several states over 30 years.

Sofie has strong values and was easily disappointed in bosses who were duplicitous. Somehow she had her share of them. By the time she was 58, she was completely burned out and didn't want to work anymore. But she still did, until, at age 62, she retired. Divorced and unfettered, she wanted to see the world.

Against advice of others about the risks of "quitting work cold turkey," she vanished from the radar of her former colleagues for over a year. After a health setback, she decided to find a job to supplement her income and create more social engagement in her life.

Now three years later, she wants to share the lessons she learned the hard way. She says, "If you want to retire, don't do it! Just slow down. If you are a high-powered woman professional, delay full retirement, and if you do stop work, stay connected. Set a plan to get what you want and need without working full-time."

Now, of course, you are further from retirement than Sophie, but what she did wrong was to leave before she had a viable plan for income and meaning from life after work.

Here's why. Do you remember the old adage, "The best time to look for a new job is while you are still employed?" My father told me this several times in my own career, and admittedly it totally irritated me when he said it. I would be pacing about the house, fretting or seething about something at work and wanting to "get out," so I would call him for a supportive ear. And every single time, he would repeat that phrase about looking, not leaping. And being in the profession of helping others move from one position to another, I would offer them the same advice, acknowledging, as I am with you, that none of us, no matter what the profession, is immune from this occasional desire to escape a bad situation by jumping ship in the night without any advance preparation. But, as you know, the truth is that having a plan and a contingency plan make for much better decisions and rewards down the road.

So, even at the point of considering a move at mid-career, you need to create your plan while you are still working. I would even venture to say that you need several possible options that you created immediately, while you are thinking about it, for execution later, once you move forward.

"Why?" you may ask, "Why do I need so many plans now?" The short answer is that at this moment, you are at the pinnacle of choice, assuming you are healthy. You have a lifetime of experiences that you could share, or you could choose something completely different. And, your mind is still largely absorbed in the world of work. Once you move to your next job, that may or may not be as true.

Your Preferred Routes – How To Decide

Oh, the Places You'll Go!, this fun career book by Dr. Suess is upbeat and optimistic about authentically pursuing options. Your route is like this also. It is a list of possible ways to get to where you want to be. For example, if I am in Maryland, where I grew up, and I want to get to Michigan, I have several options available if I drive. I can take the shortest route or one with scenery. I can stay the night in Virginia. I can take freeways, surface roads, or a combination of both.

But I need to have a map to determine my preferred route, and so do you. And this chapter will quickly and easily help you sketch out the logical plan that you can implement over time to move yourself forward.

Recognizing that emotion and style are also factors in actually travelling the route, the chapter also helps you double-check anything that could hold you back.

Story of the Radiator

When I was small, my family used to take daytrips for vacation. I always thought it was because the hotels in the new destination were full or that it must be horrible to sleep away when one only drove for three hours to get somewhere. Once in my teens, I realized that daytrips were all we could afford.

Each year we would determine where to go in a kind of family meeting. After we decided and chose the date, my Dad would begin the planning process for all the things we would need to have in the car and determine the timing and route we would use. He taught me to read a map and to provide input into how often we should stop, which freeways to take, and to calculate when we would arrive. It was exciting to help him create the journey for the whole family, and I always looked forward to it.

During the journey, I was the backseat navigator who found another route if there was a detour or serious traffic jam and who reminded him that it was time to stop—well actually, my younger sister reminded him more often than I did! Of course, GPS does this now, but you get the idea of how this planning process is similar to choosing your next job.

Anyway, one year we decided to travel from Baltimore to Atlantic City, New Jersey. I went out early in the morning to help my Dad load the car and set up the maps when there he was, with two gallon jugs of water, one in each hand. When I asked him what they were for, he replied that the radiator had been giving him some trouble, so they were in case of emergency. I was astonished because I had ridden in that car probably every day and had never known there was a problem.

As soon as he mentioned this possibility, I became nervous and vigilant. He must have sensed this anxiety because he explained to me, "Always remember that having something along in case of emergency should make you feel calm, not anxious." And so I relaxed.

We never needed the water on that trip, and it made the round-trip sitting unused in the trunk, taking up space that could have been used for another blanket or something. But I learned a valuable lesson.

This kind of "hazard insurance" is very relevant to your planning process. First, as I have mentioned in the earlier chapters, even if you remain with your employer for a while more, having a new plan developed prepares you for the day when that is no longer the case—a lot of your work and outlook will shift once your plan is developed, and this should help you stay calm and "a driver," who can decide which exit ramp to take.

Secondly, whenever we plan for a new job, situation, or career, we cannot possibly see all of the aspects that may come to be. We will know the beginning of the journey but not where the detours or traffic jams in our careers may occur. So having our own personal map with alternate routes allows us to stay calm, alert but flexible, and to feel competent to take the journey versus just sit at home and watch television.

Finding your best routes is a strategic decision and one that means you have to both brainstorm and be a little bit comfortable with ambiguity. It is important to know that we don't actually have to be entirely correct in our route planning. We just have to know how relatively far the journey is from where we are starting, what we need along the way, and when we will stop for rest.

First Steps – Taking Action To Decide Your Routes

Knowing your natural strengths, skills in demand, and work environment preferences should make you feel confident that you are in alignment with yourself and valuable to businesses, and that you will be moving forward toward a future work setting that provides meaning, prosperity, and growth for you.

It is an important first step, and you should acknowledge the power of this step. It is like putting the gas in your car—you haven't traveled anywhere, but you have the potential to do so at any time you want.

It can be tempting to stop here and just let things drift along. If not careful, career planning can "stall out" at this stage because of fear. Why would this be? Because all the "safe" work of looking inside is about finished, and now the part that feels more risky emerges.

It is a similar dynamic to what you may have noticed in your friends or colleagues—many people go around saying that they want to change their careers or jobs and complain about what they don't like, but that is where it stops. They never take the next step to look around. As a coach, I have come to see this place of fear as normal and a good sign that the person is really thinking through the implications of what they may lose by leaving their current job.

This is especially true as you consider moving out of a leadership role. Losing social relationships based on status and importance in the world takes courage. To leave all of that behind is scary and can keep you or me from acting when we know we should.

The same could happen with your plans. Without a plan to move forward in a low risk way, you may be stuck with one foot on the brake and the other on the accelerator, wanting to progress but too nervous to do it.

This is a time to reflect also on your personality and risk tolerance for change, being judged by others, and being "wrong". Depending on your personality, you can perceive less or more risk from the same situation. It's important to honor your unique approach to change, and at the same time figure out what you need to move forward. The chart below shows the needs and solutions for several personality characteristics. Please find the one closest to you and adapt the "solutions" to what will work best for you.

How Personality Impacts Successful Career Action

Personality Type	Needs in Times of Change	Solutions to Move Forward
Likes Harmony, Teamwork	Not to Disappoint Others	• Provide the "why" of your move to those you care about, and a way to stay connected afterward. • Offer assistance to others once you have succeeded. • Have a partner who can remind you that being true to yourself is the best gift you give the world.
Likes Quick Action, Decisive	Stay Patient	• Break big goals into small actions with easy success. • Have an accountability partner. • Remember the "big picture" and that inefficiency is normal.

Personality Type	Needs in Times of Change	Solutions to Move Forward
Loves Big Ideas	Translate the Idea into Actions	• Follow the Roadmap in a disciplined way. • Resist starting another path until this one is researched. • Use your intuition for timing of conversations with others. • Have a partner to "blue-sky" with who will also keep you grounded.
Perfectionist, Likes to Be Correct	Feel Successful Even When Things feel Cloudy	• Analyze actions using a risk- benefit chart, and prioritize. • Have a partner who helps grant permission to try the prioritized action, even if unproven. • Remember that inefficiency and feeling vulnerable is normal.

You probably have additional personal needs in times of change that you can add in to this chart, and I encourage you to add them. Spend a few minutes thinking of how you got through other changes in your life, because these insights will fuel your confidence to take action now. It's a good idea to find one or two trusted partners. The partners can be professional career or executive coaches, mentors you have had in life, or colleagues with deep ability to listen without judging. Of course you can do this alone without a partner as well. But my experience is that the partner helps accelerate the speed of success.

At this point, you know all you need to in order to move forward. By the way, we never know everything at the start of something new, we just need 70-80%. And even if we procrastinate, we will never know 100% until we try it. So the next section helps us set the direction for long term actions, or our ideal types of jobs.

Next – Set Your Ideal Types of Jobs in 3 Easy Steps

One: The first step is to clarify your ideal destinations.

Two: The second is to research and network. You need to do research about options that may be available to you. These can be done via the Internet or through networking, and in a low risk way. Having a list of options is like making a list of possible destinations to visit on your journey.

Three: The third is to realize that staying still is just as risky as moving forward. You must give yourself permission to pursue your "bucket list" of career positions. The reality is that eventually we will all be working less than full-time. Either our age, our ability, or our health will change, so we will need to meet that challenge by accepting that the way we do work or find meaning in the world also has to change. So planning earlier is actually less risky than staying still.

Then you should consider the future years you have left to work. If you are 50, that may be 15 to 20 years. If you are 60, it can still be 10 years plus. How do you want to spend the last decade or more of your working life? If you remain in your current position with your current employer for all that time, you are likely to diminish in importance, as others, with newer skills and fresh ideas, rise through the organization.

The next story illustrates how to think through this phase of your planning process.

Mary's Story

To illustrate what this phase of planning looks like, I'll describe Mary, a logical, strong woman who created her initial pathway in less than three hours after she had all her data. Here's what she came up with:

A senior manager I know, we'll call her Mary, has pulled herself up by her bootstraps and secured the top position in one division of a mid-sized health care company. She longs for freedom but craves security. After getting herself through the "crossroads," she realized that she had been taking on the work for others who were not willing to work as hard as she did and that because she was so organized, she was basically doing 2.5 jobs instead of one. She determined that:

- She wanted to work for 12 more years and didn't want to be in one job that whole time.

- She calculated that four years from now, she would have her house paid off and could reduce her income.
- Between now and then, she would look for a job in a similar industry where she could make the same or a little less money but work only 45 hours a week instead of 60.
- When she calculated her income tax impact and the actual amount per hour she was making, she realized that even less money annually was more per hour than her current job.

This analysis freed her to own her worth and value. From a personality standpoint, she hated the commute and wanted to have flexible hours to travel after rush hour. She also hated being middle-aged and still "evaluated" on her performance. She was organized, dependable, and getting taken advantage of because, you guessed it, she was a "pleaser" and valued service to others and belonging to a group. Her new trust in herself led her to these conclusions about the ideal work environment for her:

- A best place to work company that encouraged flextime with top performers
- A place where merit was not rewarded with extra work
- A place with a lot of talented people that did not tolerate poor performers
- A job where she could use her talent for organizing and her ability to work quickly to assist in executing the company's strategic goals
- A job that would take her 2–3 years to master, so she would not feel guilty moving on after that
- A company big enough that she could transfer to another location if she wanted to remain with them, assuming she did well
- A job in Health Care that she could flex from to another role later
- A job that paid her hourly with no overtime, but at a professional rate

What To Add In

She realized that she needed to add some things into her daily routine to look for the ideal job, even though she was completely overwhelmed with work. You know what it's like when you're going to travel—you work doubly hard finishing your work, packing, organizing, and preparing your house for your absence, and then you get ready, you have the ticket, and you've committed to go—exhausted but fulfilled.

And at that time you realize, "This is a lot more work than my regular life. I will have to do a lot more just to get myself ready, and then after I come back, I'll have more work." You basically double up on work to fit in the new preparation. This is similar.

Letting Things Go

And there are things that she had to give away. Perhaps the hardest of these was that she loved being "understood" by others and not rocking the boat. You can see from the list above that her technical knowledge made her ready for this change, but her personality was getting in the way of setting boundaries around what she was willing to do and not do.

You also will have things you'll need to give away. For example, when you get closer to the end of your career, you will likely have to give away the leadership role if you want to have relevant skills to keep working. This is because you will need to know and have a reputation for doing the work yourself, similar to what you had starting out in your career. You may need to give away being full-time in a structured organization where other people are telling you what to do. You'll have to give away the safety of other people telling you if you are good enough—and you'll need the courage to "pave your own road."

Your Turn – Summarize Your Unique Style and Preferred Routes

Step 1 – Capture all the info you have collected.

My Personal Career Roadmap	My Specifics
1. Things I would like to find in a job. Describe from your past analysis.	
2. Past dislikes from jobs—things I want to avoid in any job.	

3. My style
 	
My meaning
 	
My prosperity
 	
My growth
 	
My personality
 	
People
 	
     Ideas
 	
     Action
 	
     Process	

4. Stressors to avoid	

5. My Preferred Route
 	
   Natural talents to use
 	
      1.	

My Personal Career Roadmap	My Specifics
2.	
3.	

6. Ideal Work Setting
    Hours
    Location
    Size of company
    For-profit/Non-profit	

7. Money—amount min. and max. Benefits—years till Medicare and how to pay	
8. Freedom	
9. My talents in demand	

Step 2: Clarify Timeline for Work

Beyond having options for right now, it's important to get a sense for yourself of how long you want to work. I know—it's early for you to be thinking about this—but it's essential, so please do it.

My Current Age:

My Preferred Kinds of Work:

Age	My Ideal Work Setting	My Preference Full-time, Part-time, Freelance, None (Retired)
40-45		
46-50		
51-55		
56-60		
61-65		
66-70		
71+		

How did that analysis feel? For many it is sobering as you think about the end of work. For others, it is exciting to see that there are many different ways to work, and that it is natural that things change. Realize that even though you may think you are just making these options up with little reliable data, you can actually complete this chart fairly accurately.

Look at the amount of money you will need at each of these ages to make ends meet, assuming you keep working. Next, think conservatively about your health, stamina, and your tolerance for BS! Then, enter the ideal work environment first and put options for full-time, part-time, or freelance.

This may feel a bit serious, but taking this step is very helpful – it is what most people fail to do and what stops them from having a sense of control over their work lives. You see, you pick your ultimate destination or outcomes, and then you work backwards from that.

In the space below, write down three possible job options that you would like to pursue if the money is right, if the timing is right, and if the support system is right.

My Mid-Career Roadmap: Three Job Options

1.

2.

3.

Comments:

Think of it like you would a test drive when you go to the car lot. You know you might want a minivan, you might want a hybrid, or you might want something that is sporty—but you really don't know which model or which make you want—

until you have the proverbial test drive. In that setting, we're the customer, right? We have the money, we have the energy, we have the desire, so we're the one that's going to get the vehicle we want.

Do you realize that your career can be exactly like that? You can be the customer of your own career. You can design your career to fit you—and even if it's not perfect, it will be way closer than just letting things kind of go as they will.

This is true even if you're conservative and you don't like change. The job you're in is changing underneath you every day and is likely not sustainable in its current form for, I would say, more than two years. For anybody, especially after you've mastered your job, it will not be sustainable for you in terms of how you love it or what you like for more than two more additional years.

So let's make an agreement right now that between now and two years from now, you will make a job change. At a minimum, you will add more value or reduce stress in your current job. At the maximum, you will research and find the next job that is at the intersection of your personal meaning, prosperity, and growth. In making this change, whether small or large, you will agree to view it as your right to choose a new way to express your natural talents in the world. You agree to push through the fear if you have moments where you think you don't deserve this change or that it reflects selfishness or whimsy.

Now that you have listed everything out, we're ready to identify the three main options for women for shifting their careers to match themselves. We'll list jobs and types of schedules that you can use to create your own specific "test drives." But, before we do that in the next section, please take a moment to reflect on what you have learned about yourself and your worth, as a result of this process.

Roadmap Research

Set a Plan for Your Next 3 Jobs

Your specific routes are choices that could possibly fulfill you, either now, in a couple of years, or even longer.

Looking back at the full-time route, for example, is just the beginning of your choices. Many people assume that if they determine at mid-career to stay with the "full-time" option, they are supposed to stay with their current employer until age 66 or 67. This is certainly not the only alternative.

A sample list of what to do with each possible category is provided below for you to reference. Remember, you are just planning the next move, *not* all the moves from now to not working.

Full-time Category Options	Potential Benefits	Potential Drawbacks	Comments
Same employer, same job	-Financial security -Know the culture -Use current skills -Current relationships -Already known entity	-Possible boredom -Lower energy than job demands -Same hours -Increase in years spent here vs. gaining new experience	The remainder of the time with the present employer means that you delay your new life. Your new career is like the "car in the garage" that doesn't get driven.
Same employer, different job	-Financial security -Known entity -New challenge with little relative risk -Possible lower stress	-May require new learning -Possibly more hours for a while -New boss and relationships to adjust to	If there is a job in your organization that matches your desired environment, this option can provide you with the experience of moving without the bigger adjustment of a new company.

Full-time in a similar job but with a different company	-Choice of size of company -New experience -Benefits and financial stability -Use current skills	-Time to learn and adjust -New is not always better -May require new learning and possibly new hours -New boss and peers to adjust to	This move can keep you very active and challenged while remaining in a "safe" full-time situation. Always pursue the new opportunity before leaving the old one.
Full-time in a different job with a different company	-Can be a true encore career, changing course -Can be fun to learn new information and skills -Can set you on a new path for the next 10–15 years -Can be related to skills you have but have not used much	-Planning and learning prior to getting the job required -May feel like starting over to move from mastery to neophyte -May feel a real sense of fear that you may not succeed	The good news here is that you expand your life significantly. If you have health, energy, and interest, this move can rejuvenate you. The risk is a bit higher, but remember that you are just trying it out for 2 years or so.

Figure out what marker you will use—when is the earliest you may leave a full-time job, assuming you have an option that brings the MPG (meaning, prosperity, growth) you have identified?

a. Once you determine the earliest time, identify the longest time you think you will still work (use the number of years between now and when you are 70 to calculate this if you are in good health).

b. This is your range of planning time or the distance from where you are today to where you are going next.

c. Plan backward from the soonest time to the present, and begin listing key mile markers you need to see to be ready to take the exit ramp.

Roadblocks and Accelerators

Support from Colleagues and Family – This can be either a roadblock or an accelerator. Though our planning is largely logical, the emotional cushion we need to grow and change is equally important. So it is essential that we include the powerful influence that family and colleagues can have on our choices at mid-career and beyond. Though it is different from earlier in life, in that we actually know what works for us and doesn't, our sense of needing acceptance and being understood by those close to us requires that we add the communications and boundaries that will be needed into our planning process. The influence of these others can be either an accelerator or a brake at this point. Here's an illustration.

Stephanie

Stephanie worked in a large Fortune 5 business for 35 years. She started right after college and was now 57 years old. She noted, "I am in the no-man's land between the career I loved and an uncertain future. My husband doesn't understand why I might want a change because he thinks that I should build up income for our future security. But I have done the same kind of work so long that I feel like I deserve some freedom to choose. Right now I should have some fun in life. There are no guarantees, you know. What if I give away my life to this job, then I am too old and frail to have fun later? I am more than a work unit. I moved up the tough way when women had to work harder than men just to be in the room. I've done a lot and want more for this time in my life."

I was alarmed that when I described this to my women colleagues, they thought I was selfish. Now, I just don't know what to do. I guess I'll have to choose between moving ahead anyway and risking their disdain, or staying in a safe and well-understood world that I absolutely resent.

==================

Stephanie's story show us the need to have courage and to realize that just because there are not a lot of role models for what we want to achieve, we shouldn't feel trepidation. Once again, we are our own role models, almost like it was back in the 70s and early 80s when we were so misunderstood in the workplace. Remember that feeling? I want you to realize that by having courage and moving forward anyway, it all worked out.

The most important aspect is to find people to talk to who do support you. The others who are skeptical will need to wait to endorse your decision until they see the results. But please do not wait for their approval before moving forward. If you do, you'll be waiting a long time. Reassure the skeptics that you care about them and you are being logical, but don't expect them to be convinced or supportive. And try not to resent the extra work you take on by having to communicate more than you want to.

In order to use this insight, it is helpful to make a "mind shift." For successful mid-career change, I'm asking you to "turn a switch in your head" that broadens your definition of success, beyond whatever career model you have been following. It is relatively easy if you just decide to do it. Like a manual gearshift on your car, it allows you more control and a personalized experience.

The secret is to majorly shift from thinking of a career as something that you own, that you have to build and always make bigger, that will sustain itself indefinitely and that will always grow, to realize that things actually change significantly somewhere around mid-career. Though you can still achieve and create bigger challenges if you wish, you also have the ability and right to change it up fairly radically, even downshifting. In a way, this broader mindset provides you an opportunity to change paths to a different concept of your career than you had earlier in life.

And getting it straight in your head makes you capable of describing this to friends and family without too much second-guessing of yourself. It's important to have conviction in order to have a purposeful life. No one else will grant it to you. And your belief in yourself and your plan, with contingencies in case things don't work out perfectly, will reassure your close ones that you have not gone completely crazy.

Now, it is possible that after your examination and by looking at everything, you change your mind about your current job and decide that it's actually perfect. But I guarantee you that the things you wrote down that you really dislike (unless you go to your boss and tell him or her about specific changes that are agreed to and successfully implemented) pretty soon you will be back in the same space where you were at the time you decided that it was time to make a change. Even though I am optimistic every time a client decides to stick it out and take this "less risky" option, I must admit that most of the time, they call me a month or two later to report that things are back at "square one."

Phase 3 –
Use Your Roadmap

3 – Use Your Roadmap	• Getting Ready To Use Your Roadmap • Acquire the Courage To Act • Short-Term Actions To Move Forward • Use the "Rules of the Road" • Roadblock and Accelerators • Summary Conclusion

PART 1:
Getting Ready
To Use Your Roadmap

Between having a plan and actually using it, there is a big, foggy area. You know well how many times you intend to do something in life but actually making the time and effort takes way more energy and courage than you think it will. The same is true here. Having your roadmap is about 70% of the work, but using it, that last 30% can feel like an enormous leap. Though you know that the roadmap makes sense, your emotions and the feeling of overwhelm that just surviving day to day sometimes inspires can make things difficult. We will focus on four areas that will help you through the fog.

The four important abilities are: acquiring the courage to act, choosing job options, using the career "rules of the road," committing short term for only 2–3 years to each job, and getting past your roadblocks and using accelerators to a confident journey.

Acquire the Courage To Act

The first and most challenging part of using your roadmap is acquiring the courage to act. This challenge is not new to any career changer, but I want you to know that it should logically be less of an issue for you at mid-career than at any other time of your working life.

A Personal Story

Many years ago, though I had been in a super job for several years, I found myself completely frustrated. I had taken the job for security and was lucky enough that it used my skills well and was in a positive environment for the most part. But despite my best intentions to remain happy and content, I just couldn't do it. It just felt too long to be doing the same thing, and I got to the point where I was feeling old before my time. Can you relate to this? I had a lot of fears and the work was absorbing, so I didn't have the additional energy left to find a new job and had decided to just continue with my current job, hoping that when I felt better, I'd find a new, full-time job that paid better.

However, what I was doing no longer gave me as much meaning. Additionally, I felt like I couldn't really compete as well as I needed to.

So I started to research. Rather than going onto job websites like monster.com, I chose to talk to people—friends, family members, ex-colleagues—to learn more about their jobs and work experiences. And it is through so many of these conversations that I gathered the most valuable information to help me make an informed and exciting job change.

I ended up going back out on my own consulting career full time. I was scared but exhilarated. And I was completely misunderstood by those who only categorized people into full-time and part-time workers. But luckily I had a plan and was flexible, so things worked out for me.

This story is not to tell you that I am smart, but that if I can do it, you can too. Find a path and try it out. And in doing so, you will realize that what you have been doing is no better for you than making a change.

"Sometimes you have to move backward to move ahead."

PART 2:
Short-Term Actions
to Move Forward

Actions you can take in your current job

- Training, projects, mentoring, discussions with boss, networking

These actions have minimal risk and can prepare you for larger changes step by step.

Actions you can take through research

- Technical knowledge, other opportunities, industries
- Talk to people you know and interview them about their work.
- Read books or watch DVDs. These can be about any interest area linked to your career or to your hobbies.

- Join professional associations. These usually meet once per month, and you can gain exposure to others in your line of work, plus have some fun!

These actions require a bit more overt commitment to others that you are looking for something new, but have the advantage of possibly resulting in an actual job opportunity.

Actions you can take through education

- Certificates, educational assistance, online
- Volunteer in a cause that you find interesting or worthwhile. You can get a lot of useful experience.

These actions are "under the radar" but again prepare you for larger opportunities later.

Actions you can take in your non-worklife

- Hobbies, trips, exploration, discussions with family and friends
- Cultivate hobbies that you are interested in.
- Create space in your life for work-life balance.

These actions build up the meaning and balance in your life and prepare you for reducing the amount that work determines your identity.

PART 3:
Use the Career "Rules of the Road"

For this section, I have adapted the "rules of the road" for effective and safe driving. The reason is that it's a fun way to think about moving forward safely and confidently into any new path. If you're of the same generation as me, you probably learned these in driving school.

1. Aim high in steering – look as far ahead as you can.
2. Keep your eyes moving – search and scan, glancing left and right.
3. Get the big picture – know what's going on around you, total awareness.
4. Make sure others see you! – communicate.
5. Leave yourself an out – an escape path if necessary.

These rules were designed as the Smith System in 1952.[5] It was the first professional driver training company in the United States. I think their rules became universally applied for many driving schools later. And I know that those same rules, translated to your mid-career search, apply for you today.

Let's examine each rule briefly to see how it can help us.

1. Aim High in Steering – Look as Far Ahead as You Can

---

[5] smith-system.com

In order to see things coming and watch out for obstacles or unusual conditions that may occur, we need to look further ahead than tomorrow, next week, or even next month if possible. Why? Because several major things are changing dynamically throughout the course of any job tenure.

- The outlook for our jobs – Is our desired new job becoming more in demand? Are lots of other people crowding it where before it was a specialty field?
- Are you likely to need to shift in order to stay on track?
- Will you need new skills to pursue the job you want to get?

The reason to know these things is to have predictability and to make good decisions. Too many of us just do what we are told, even after we have been working 25 or 30 years or more. By looking far ahead, we avoid waiting for others to give us the "green light" on what to do.

2. Keep Your Eyes Moving – Glance Left and Right

This seems easy, right? When driving, we have to look left and right because traffic is unpredictable and it comes from both sides—or sometimes there are pedestrians on the road, accidents, emergency vehicles, or bicyclists. When it comes to a new job search, this equals:

- Asking for feedback on what people find valuable about your skills

- Networking with your colleagues outside your normal job
- Keeping up to date on new trends and opportunities

Keeping track of what is happening keeps your job search plan relevant and useful, and keeps you motivated to implement it.

3. Get the Big Picture – Know What's Going On Around Your Vehicle as You Drive. Total awareness.

- The outlook for economic conditions—is it sunny or stormy for jobs in your area of capability?
- Is there increased competition and politics for who gets ahead and how they do it?
- Are a lot of people in your age group retiring, and, if so, how happy are they?
- Are people successfully moving from employee to sole proprietor?
- Who are they and what skills do they possess that let them do this? How prosperous and happy are they?

You need to know the answers to these questions to get the big picture of trends in employment. For example, if in the last year, 12 people of 50 that you know retired and those 12 are now all beating down your door telling you how wonderful it is, that's important. But If they are trying to get a consulting gig after being invisible for some time, that's important in a different way.

4. Make Sure Others See You – Communicate!

Most clients of mine have to learn this skill. I have a confession—I had to learn it too! The need to promote oneself is unattractive to most women professionals. However, it's not unattractive to men professionals. I wondered why. In researching this difference, I found out that men are taught from a young age that they are supposed to openly compete and to differentiate themselves, whereas the societal expectation of women is, you guessed it, to fit in and be nice, of service, useful, and dependable.

Initially this just made sense, but then it made me seriously angry. After that, I realized that this is part of the "having it all" recipe that we, as women in the 70s and 80s, didn't get. We learned that we needed to work harder and be smarter. But that is not enough. And at mid-career and beyond, being seen is even more important.

Why? You know the answer to this if you are going through menopause or about to. At some point in that process, you will or have been treated as "invisible" by men and by other women. You know the feeling. Whereas you used to walk in a store and be greeted enthusiastically, now you may not be greeted at all. So it's important to hone this skill, as you get ready for a job search.

Here are some easy actions that indicate you are making sure others see you.

- Be unpredictable—Don't always acquiesce.
- Have presence—Walk in a room like you own it.

- Ask for what you want in scheduling or tasks while still in your current role.
- Instead of bringing data to a meeting, ask questions of others about their thinking.
- "Call out" faulty thinking in a neutral way, not in an emotional or "hurt" way.
- Hold at least one networking coffee per month with new people you want to learn from and connect with.
- Join Linked In and make sure you comment on groups you join.

5. Leave Yourself an Out – Know Your Escape Path if Necessary

This one is essential for your next series of jobs. We know by now that nothing stays the same, and we are embracing the idea that we will change jobs several more times. So, we need a "next plan" or escape path.

I've watched as super talented women let the end of a job happen (especially those who had contracts or political appointments where the potential end was known a year in advance) because they didn't want to be disloyal. If you read this and think, "How ridiculous that someone would do that!" well, have some compassion and don't judge too harshly. Not only do all the successful women I know have a deep dedication to their work, but they also have a strong commitment to the people they are working with.

The truth is that every job changes over time, and all companies do too. And, therefore, whatever is working for you in your current job will change either to be more in concert with what is good for you—or less. Staying the same, especially after five years in one job, is very unlikely. Your job is to have the contingency plan (or escape plan) thought of while things are good, NOT after things go badly.

Just like in the driver's ed class, when shown a road with a "curve ahead" sign, the instructor asks, "Where is your escape path?" if you are like me, you look to the side of the road to see if there is a shoulder. But what if there isn't one? You may have to go into the passing lane, cross the road to the other shoulder if you can do it safely, OR slow down or exit the road another way. The thing you don't do is sit in someone's blind spot, matching them and hoping they give in first.

Of all the women I have known and all the research I have done, I have found that underneath this lack of thinking ahead is the sense that if we are looking away from the job, we are "cheating" on the employer. Let's get over it. If you are one of the 10% who don't have this problem, great! If not, realize that the employer isn't planning your future, but to be successful and of most value to any organization, someone has to be working on it. So rather than feel like you are cheating, realize that you are "doing your job" by planning for the next one.

Here are some easy actions you can take to leave yourself an out:

- Talk to your current boss about other opportunities in your company that could use your natural skills.
- Get a business license for your solopreneur company. You don't have to use it right away.
- Pick a skill you are naturally talented at and learn all you can about jobs using that skill.
- Keep in touch with people you have worked with in past jobs.
- Learn about informational interviews and set some up using networks to learn about new opportunities in other industries.
- Get certified in something not necessary for your current job; for example, as a copywriter, financial professional, construction project manager, research writer, coach, values specialist, tutor, etc.
- Network with others who do the job on their own and learn the ups and downs of the solo life.
- Volunteer with non-profits that value your help and that you enjoy.

Roadblocks and Accelerators

Accelerator – Expect Deviations

A recent study showed that 43% of people 30 and older wanted to have a new career, but that most of them had 3–5 obstacles stopping them. These barriers included worries about financial security, not knowing what to do instead of their current job, concern about not having the proper skills or education, and worrying about being too old or experienced in their jobs.

I guess this shows that it's normal to wait and worry about the risk of taking on a new position, and, as a result, we let ourselves increasingly feel stale and stuck in our current ones. But though these fears are understandable, I think you'll agree that this is a pretty stupid way to live, especially if you are talented and have portable skills.

We, women, in particular, have other, less logical obstacles that we experience but usually "push down" or don't look at. These include the fraud factor, losing friends, failing, and being seen as a quitter. They're really powerful inhibitors that we need to get past—to do that, let's look at them for what they are.

Roadblock – The Fraud Factor

While not confined to women, the idea behind the "fraud factor" is that many of us live in fear of being uncovered as being less intelligent or talented than we hope we are. This fear rears its ugly head most often in times of life transition, crisis, or when we are thinking of starting over in a new job or profession.

One of the most talented women I know, Katherine, was outwardly completely confident and hit all obstacles in stride. She was the last person you would ever think would have this fear. But when her old boss left the company and brought in his own second in command, she knew she had to leave but became frozen with self-doubt. In helping her sort out this unexpected fear, she realized that she had never felt she "had" to leave a job before—she had always been the one to go. Somehow being out of control stirred up a feeling of fear that she hadn't known she would have.

Roadblock – Losing Friends

There's a saying that you find out who your true friends are when you do badly or when you do better than they do. I'll go even further. For professional women, we connect our worth not only to what we do for the organization, but to who approves of and likes us. As soon as we push past barriers and either go our own way or move ahead of others, we know . . . KNOW . . . that others who were friendly will "put us in a box" of their own interpretation and we will feel a distance that is uncomfortable. I'm sure you've been there.

No matter how much we want to blithely ignore and minimize it, we feel loss anyway. And mostly we hate ourselves for falling prey to that. Many of the women I know say that they even feel badly about being disliked by someone they consider "an asshole." And when you change your job, those few people will come out of the woodwork and say things about you to distance themselves from you. Realize this is normal and unavoidable, and not something that should hold you back.

Roadblock – Being a "Quitter"

Leaving a job means giving up on it. Period. Even if it's to move to something better. It's logical and makes sense, right? So why do we worry about acknowledging it? In talking with other women, it's because we don't want to make people still in that job feel like losers or that we are acting like we are superior to others. Okay, maybe you have escaped this fate— but, if not, realize that quitting/leaving is necessary to growth. As an old Lincoln Park song says, "Every new beginning comes from some other beginning's end."

Getting Past Roadblocks – Our Mindset Needs To Shift

How do we go from waiting, hanging on, and being frustrated and worried to taking action right now? We only need to change our minds.

Think of your career and current job as a vehicle for self-expression. At the beginning of each job, it's like a shiny new car, moped, or bike. It's something we are proud of and enhances how we feel about ourselves. Then something changes- it always does- and we're either bored, finding it takes too much "maintenance," or we have the proverbial "crash" and our career vehicle isn't so pretty anymore.

What would you do if your vehicle was messed up, a clunker? Would you wait and say, "I'm not good enough for a better car?" Of course, you wouldn't.

Waiting too long to look for your next job is like saying, "Hey, there's a lot of traffic on the highway right now. I think I'll go out and sit in it a while." We'd never do such a ludicrous thing. But most of us do that in our careers. It's like Isaac Newton's first law of Motion, the law of inertia—you know—a body in motion stays in motion, but a body at rest stays at rest.

It's up to you to decide that it's time to move forward. It's riskier to wait than to plan for something new, for several reasons. First, there is "aging in place." If you have been in the same job for more than five years, you are at risk for being like a ripening cheese. After you've mastered your current job, you are likely re-learning the same things over and over, kind of like in the 1993 movie *Groundhog Day*. At the beginning, it feels okay, like you are so talented that you can predict everything that is happening to you.

That would be great, except for a concept called "opportunity cost." Every month or year that you spend beyond your mastery of a job is time you are letting get away from you for other bright, interesting, fun, new things you could be learning. At mid-career, you may just feel it as an increased tendency for jealousy when you hear about someone else's new venture. But realize that the comparison is NOT the worst part.

The worst part is that your skills and mind are slowly declining invisibly, and you will not see it until later. It's like the depreciating asset of a car—as soon as it's driven off the lot, it is worth less than it was prior to sitting in it. Do you want your assets to depreciate? Certainly not!

Summary –
Your Route, Your Speed, Your Style™

"Packing" for the Journey

Depending on what paths you have chosen, you will have different amounts and durations of preparation for the journey. For example, even if you keep your current job and want to prepare for part-time freelance side work later, you have a lot of preparing to do. You would need about 2–4 months of planning with 3–6 hours per week. This is a reasonable estimate given that new things take more time to get done than you think they should. You'd need to figure out your niche, evaluate your certificate and licenses and update them if necessary, get a business license, tax certificate and bank account, complete a document showing your company that your work will not compete with them, build a web page, do some soft marketing, and set your rates and ideal client profile. You'd also need to communicate to any affected person in your life why you are doing this and to ask for their support.

This may seem like a lot, but that's only until you break down the work over time and priority. At this point in the process, an action planning chart is essential.

Here's another example. A colleague who was a gifted Montessori teacher for almost 30 years wanted to keep working but give up time in the classroom. She found a licensure for "mentors" for other Montessori teachers and researched it. It cost a bit of money and took her two years of training, testing, and using the knowledge, but now she has the job she wants for her later career. Through the two years, she may have been overwhelmed at times and that would be normal, but she had her timeline and action plan and just adapted it to keep moving forward.

Your Turn

Use the "action planning" chart to record the routes to your goals, so that you can compare and contrast the attractiveness of the various options you are considering.

For each action you listed:

1. Prioritize (how important is it compared to the other actions?)
2. Set the timing (when will you start compared with the other actions?)
3. Set due dates and a time to check on your progress
4. Identify resources you need to get started
5. Plan how to make time in your week/calendar
6. Communicate your plan to others affected

In the next 5 years, I will feel successful in my career by doing the following things:

New – Traveling "uphill"

Stay on the same path – Taking the "freeway"

Checking out – Taking the "scenic route"

Once you've thought through the routes and goals, you're ready to complete the initial planning process.

My Action Planning Career Chart

Action	Priority	Timing/Due Dates	Resources	How to make time/ how much time
1.				
2.				
3.				
4.				
5.				
6.				

Move Forward Confidently!

Now that you have committed to trading in your current job, take a second and congratulate yourself! Do you realize that though there will be tough moments between now and your next "gig," the very hardest work is already done?

YAY! Tell someone who you don't have to worry will let the secret out too soon—a coach is safe. Beyond that, who? Well, this is where things get a little sticky. You certainly cannot tell your current co-worker-friends. Don't tell your mom or dad, your sister (unless she is in a monastery somewhere), or your spouse/special someone. You can tell your dog, cat, or fish. Or you can tell me! I promise to keep it locked up till you are ready to move forward.

WHY? You can't tell others just yet because it's like posting a picture of you with a red Ferrari on Facebook before you have actually bought it. It has unintended consequences. And the worst of those could mean that you will give up in embarrassment or despair.

It's way better to journal or complete a workbook with a guide than to let your newfound freedom become visible too soon. I remember once when I was about to leave a job—it paid well, it had status and reach, and it was at a very large organization. But I was unhappy—too much politics and too many hours making small talk for someone like me, a borderline introvert. Did I let on? Of course not. I was predictable to the organization, dependable, positive, and value-added, right up until my last day.

Conclusion

Now that you have your plan and have begun to execute it, pat yourself on the back! Congratulations!

Starting down a new path feels awesome, and I know you are ready. You just have to remember a few key things in order to keep moving and to use your roadmap, with adjustments annually or so, for many years. The first is to stay confident no matter what happens externally.

Janel's Lesson

Janel was an energetic, vibrant, and upbeat woman. She was a highly decorated veteran too, a person, who had respect from all quarters in her life. She was approached by a good friend who had become the president of an influential economic development organization to develop programs for the military.

Honored to be asked to serve in a position of authority by someone she respected, Janel took the job, no questions asked. Once on the job, she attacked it with vigor and creativity, coming up with interesting new programs and concepts that would bring revenue and a great reputation to the group.

Everything was great for about a year, or, at least, it appeared to be. Janel was credited with renewing interest in military programs as a means of economic development. But then the truth came out. The organization was losing members at a hazardous rate. The revenue that was supposed to be put back into program development was moved to pay normal operating expenses. When Janel spoke up to try to prevent this, her old friend shunned her. In meetings, Janel was openly criticized no matter what she said. Hurt and confused by this, Janel tried to build support for her ideas. Nothing seemed to work.

By six months from that time, you wouldn't recognize Janel as the upbeat, positive, and creative person she really was. She had turned into a cynical, whining, and resentful person, who hated to go to work. She had gone from having self-confidence to self-doubt, and her value to the organization had eroded entirely.

It took Janel another year before she left the organization. Even though she was terribly unhappy, she wouldn't give up and quit. She spent her time seeking validation of her utility, all the while sinking deeper and deeper into feelings of futility.

As an outsider reading this story, you can easily wonder what was wrong with Janel. Why didn't she notice that it was the organization that was sick and not her? Why didn't she cut her losses and leave? Why did she allow herself to be transformed into a complaining, invisible person?

It's because she didn't evaluate the organization as unhealthy. She lived through the events as they unfolded without analyzing what they meant.

Most of us are like Janel. We know something is not right, but we have nothing to compare it with. Remember this story when you want to pretend that a job situation will get better on its own. Instead, get going and move forward. And if we try a new approach, we should not always expect that those we leave behind will be kind and fair.

How To Stay Flexible and Handle Roadblocks

Anticipate Detours and Other Roadwork

Courage is an antidote to fear.

—Anonymous

What are the roadblocks in this phase?

Expecting everything to go according to plan—Especially if you are a logical thinker, you may plan for the first few months of something new and then expect that if things go awry, it means that you have made a mistake in taking the new job or career move. But that's a trap. To accelerate your growth, expect things to happen that are not on your plan, and plan to "go around them."

The (normal) inability to foresee the eventualities that may occur—Especially since you are planning for multiple jobs over time, you cannot see all the eventualities that will occur—no one can—you may change your mind, find something you love more, or find too many costs to a path you have chosen. So you will need a way to have a backup plan. The secret to success is to know this is normal and positive (as opposed to considering it a problem). By having a backup plan, you will free yourself from frustration and anxiety.

Not being disciplined—You need to work on your future for at least half an hour daily, during lunch, before work, etc. If you don't make time for the future, your plan will sit in a drawer unused. Once on a new path, you need to check in with your feelings, successes, and learning at least once a quarter to keep yourself on a smooth road.

Interference and guilt from loved ones—This roadblock is very difficult to handle because you will have to continue to communicate purposefully, even after you have taken a new job or gone freelance. One of the unexpected challenges that can occur is that your loved ones may want you to keep defending your decision—even if they were supportive at the time. So be careful about how you "market" your change to them. Tell them the role they can play to best support you and don't be afraid of doing this. That is, you will need to clarify your work boundaries and your analysis, try to enroll your partner or spouse, and then repeatedly "sell" the plan. Because it will be new and unpredictable for your loved ones, you will need to treat it like a marketing plan (17 times per message to stick).

By listing all the possible obstacles now, you can call yourself successful in your new career roadmap!

Review and Update

It's important to make your plan a living thing that you consult regularly and finetune, like the engine of a car. You need to see it as something you maintain. The risk of avoiding its maintenance is that you once again find yourself out of control of your own worklife. That is the biggest risk most of us face in career change and one that is easily avoided.

How To Review

Readjust or finetune your plan on an ongoing basis by setting a date with yourself every quarter to celebrate your achievements and to keep your energy up by taking small steps toward your goals.

Role Modeling and Assisting Others

Having a roadmap is such a positive thing that perhaps you will have friends asking you how you did it and to share your methods with them. I hope you do.

But just remember, the path that worked for you will not necessarily work for them. The process will work, however. Your role will be to help them to accelerate, to trust themselves, and to learn how to authentically communicate to their loved ones in an effective way.

They say that the biggest learning comes from helping and mentoring others. I urge you to try it out when you have the opportunity.

I am proud of you and wish you "all green lights" on your future work journeys.